YELLOWSTONE
NATIONAL PARK

THE FIRST 150 YEARS

YELLOWSTONE
NATIONAL PARK
THE FIRST 150 YEARS

LP
LYONS
PRESS

JEFF HENRY

LYONS
PRESS

An imprint of Globe Pequot, the trade division of
The Rowman & Littlefield Publishing Group, Inc.
4501 Forbes Blvd, Ste 200, Lanham, MD 20706
www.rowman.com

Distributed by NATIONAL BOOK NETWORK

British Library Cataloguing in Publication Information available

Library of Congress Cataloging-in-Publication Data
Names: Henry, Jeff, author.
Title: Yellowstone National Park : the first 150 years / Jeff Henry.
Description: Guilford, Connecticut : Lyons Press, [2022] | Contents: The Geologic
  History—Indians—Early Explorers and Mountain Man—The Prospecting Era—Official
  Explorers—The Establishment of the Park and its Early Years—Between the Wars—Surge
  (1946–1988)—Explosive Visitation (1989–2022)—The Future.
Identifiers: LCCN 2021027521 (print) | LCCN 2021027522 (ebook) | ISBN 9781493059621
  (hardcover) | ISBN 9781493064922 (epub)
Subjects: LCSH: Yellowstone National Park—History.
Classification: LCC F722 .H475 2021 (print) | LCC F722 (ebook) | DDC 978.7/52—dc23
LC record available at https://lccn.loc.gov/2021027521
LC ebook record available at https://lccn.loc.gov/2021027522

♾™ The paper used in this publication meets the minimum requirements of American
National Standard for Information Sciences—Permanence of Paper for Printed Library
Materials, ANSI/NISO Z39.48-1992.

CONTENTS

Legendary Yellowstone photographer Frank J. Haynes shot this picture of a horse-drawn carriage passing through the Roosevelt Arch in Gardiner, Montana. The arch was built in 1903, and famously was dedicated by President Theodore Roosevelt himself when he made a visit to Yellowstone in the spring of that year. FRANK J. HAYNES, YELLOWSTONE NATIONAL PARK COLLECTION

FOREWORD

IN 2022, YELLOWSTONE NATIONAL PARK celebrates its 150th anniversary. Historical photo books appear like clockwork at anniversaries of noteworthy geographical places, and, of course, Yellowstone is such a place. My friend Jeff Henry's *Yellowstone National Park: The First 150 Years* is a vast collection of historic photos that most people have never had the privilege of seeing—until now.

Jeff has lived in and worked many jobs in the Yellowstone region for more than forty-five years. He has not only studied the literature of Yellowstone but also has become an expert photographer himself and today nourishes a collection of over 250,000 carefully cataloged pictures. He lives just north of the Grand Old Park in Paradise Valley, where he still works as a winterkeeper who just finished his forty-fifth winter in Yellowstone. From his first winter in the old Snow Lodge kitchen, where he saw guys like Bill Berg and Herb Vaughn winterkeeping, Jeff thought it was the coolest thing he had ever seen. And forty-five winters later, he still thinks the same way.

Jeff's own history is intrinsically tied to the history of Yellowstone. From Paradise Valley, he hikes the country, on-trail or off, and reads its literature incessantly. From its history-making beginnings to presidential visits, Jeff knows the ins and outs of the park's storied 150 years as a national treasure.

Jeff arrived in Yellowstone from Pennsylvania in 1977 to work as a dishwasher at Old Faithful for only three weeks before receiving a truly lucky promotion to Fishing Guide at Bridge Bay Marina, and then, like me, he never really left. Despite previously knowing of each other, we formally met in the winter of 1979-80 while he was working in the Transportation Division of T. W. Services as a snowcoach driver, and it did not take me long to learn that he was fascinating to talk to and definitely a kindred Yellowstone spirit.

In the summer of 1984, after more than a decade with the park concessioner, I returned to the National Park Service, this time as a law-enforcement ranger, and I learned soon afterward that Jeff was immersed in working for NPS on a coyote study and seasonally with the Interagency Grizzly Bear Study Team. Later, Jeff attended an NPS law-enforcement school and became a ranger himself, then starting to shoot photographs of many locations in the park.

"You know, Lee, there are two kinds of people in the world—those who live at [Yellowstone] Lake, and those who wish they did," he often said to me.

In the high-adventure summer of 1988—Yellowstone's Summer of Fire that burned more than 790,000 acres in the park—our work together cemented our common desire to stay in the park forever. That summer, Jeff had been perfectly assigned to take photographs of the park and its fires, while both on- and off-duty; those photos are now in the park's archives. As a coup, that autumn, Jeff served as lead photographer for Jim Carrier's book *Summer of Fire*.

In 1991, as I moved over to the Park Archives, Jeff's success with his photographs exploded. His photos were published in hundreds of magazines and books, on posters, and in calendars. The NPS Public Affairs Office sought him out to accompany tour groups for both informational and photographic purposes, for actual photo assignments, and to guide commercial and non-commercial film crews, including the BBC.

In *Yellowstone National Park: The First 150 Years*, Jeff has produced a book that illustrates all of Yellowstone's history, beginning with its geological history and continuing up to the present. Charts, maps, historic photos, and paintings are all arranged according to the progression of Yellowstone's historic chapters. Accompanying these visuals is rich text highlighting the park's storied history—information that will no doubt pique your interest and lead you to further investigate the park's history that Jeff himself so much appreciates.

Lee H. Whittlesey
Historian, Yellowstone National Park,
National Park Service (Retired)

INTRODUCTION

I AM KEENLY AWARE of how fortunate I have been to spend so much time in Yellowstone—by the time this book is published, I will have been in Yellowstone for almost one-third of its existence as a park. I have been privileged, indeed, to enjoy the experiences I've had. In addition to the day-to-day—often moment-to-moment—thrills and inspirations my observations have brought, I realize I've been witnessing the history of the park unfold right in front of my eyes. At times the events have been dramatic, such as when I watched the great fires of 1988 transform the park from what I had known into something different, or when I had the opportunity to shoot photographs of the original wolves destined to be reintroduced into Yellowstone after their species had been absent from the park for some seventy-odd years. I even managed a group shot of all fourteen of those pioneering wolves as they were tranquilized and laid out in rows on a garage floor near Hinton, Alberta, in preparation for their airplane flight from Canada to the United States.

There have been other dramatic transitions, too. I watched the growth of winter visitation in Yellowstone progress from small-scale to overwhelming, and then saw new regulations cut that visitation to a much lower and much more closely managed level. But everyday natural events are history, too—watching the ice seasonally freeze and melt on Yellowstone Lake, or observing the date when the first mountain bluebirds arrive in the geyser basins in the spring, or watching the bison rut in the heat and dust of late summer, and then the elk rutting in frosty meadows in autumn. A vicarious thrill consumes me whenever I watch first-time visitors arrive in the park, sensing their special excitement that can be felt only once, when seeing such a marvelous place for the first time. Those events and many others are part of Yellowstone's ongoing history, too, and any of us can watch that history develop if we spend a little time and exercise a bit of patience.

Yellowstone was designated the world's first national park on March 1, 1872. Originally intended to protect its unique array of geysers and other geothermal wonders, as well as to protect the two great falls and the colorful Grand Canyon of the Yellowstone River, the park was not at first regarded as a wildlife refuge. That soon changed, however, when the vast herds of wildlife that existed elsewhere in the West in 1872 were swiftly exterminated as the American frontier expanded to its closure in the final decades of the nineteenth century. Within a short time, the wildlife enclosed and protected within Yellowstone's boundaries began its evolution to world-renowned status as the most striking element in what many present-day observers describe as the most intact ecosystem left in the temperate portions of the world.

Needless to say, Yellowstone has gone through a large number of evolutions in its 150-year history. One of the first was its transition from an undeveloped wilderness in 1872 to a pleasuring ground for tourists just a few years later. That transition included the layout and construction of the road network we still follow today, as well as the building of hotel and restaurant accommodations and other services—including several establishments that still exist. Socially, Yellowstone National Park evolved from being a hunting ground for rugged mountain men to a destination for the well-to-do, and then later to a playground for the working- and middle-class population. There were other evolutions, too, such as the profound change in transportation—from horse-powered conveyances to internal combustion engines—that occurred in 1915 and 1916. Of course, the park is still evolving on many different fronts as we enter the middle decades of the twenty-first century.

And it is important to remember that in the long sweep of history, Yellowstone National Park is a new invention. The area had been crossed and used by early Euro-American explorers and trappers for nearly seven decades before the park was officially explored and legally designated, but that is nothing compared to the experience of the area's first human inhabitants. The Native Americans that explorers found when they initially scouted the Yellowstone area were descended from people who had been thriving here for at least 13,000 years before the explorers showed up. We know this from artifacts dated to that age that were wrought from obsidian sourced within the present-day park. Such artifacts have been found both inside and outside Yellowstone's boundaries. Native burials have also been discovered in and near Yellowstone, including one dating back to that 13,000-year mark that was found a short distance north of the park.

Even the experience of Native Americans in Yellowstone is infinitesimally brief when compared to the park's geologic history. The rocks that form the basement of the park and its surrounding area are Precambrian granites and gneisses, and are in the range of 2.7 billion years old (to put their age in perspective, they are almost two-thirds as old as the earth itself). These ancient rocks are most easily seen in the northeastern margins of Yellowstone National Park. Vastly more recent is the last explosion of the great Yellowstone caldera, a defining event in the park's geologic history that happened a mere 640,000 years ago. And most recent of all are the geothermal depositions that are even today forming new rocks in Yellowstone. The importance of geology in the Yellowstone story cannot be overstated. Geology is not only the underlying reason for the park's creation in the first place; it is also the foundation and the backdrop for all the biological and cultural events that have ever transpired, up to and including those transpiring today.

This book is an attempt to review all of Yellowstone's history and prehistory by using historical and contemporary photos, historical art, and maps and charts. As much interpretive information as possible, in the form of written text, has also been included to explain the approximately 325 illustrations in this book. It goes without saying that a work of such length and limitations can only cursorily touch upon Yellowstone's long and complex history, but it is hoped that the book may succeed in inspiring you to further investigate the park's storied past and fascinating present.

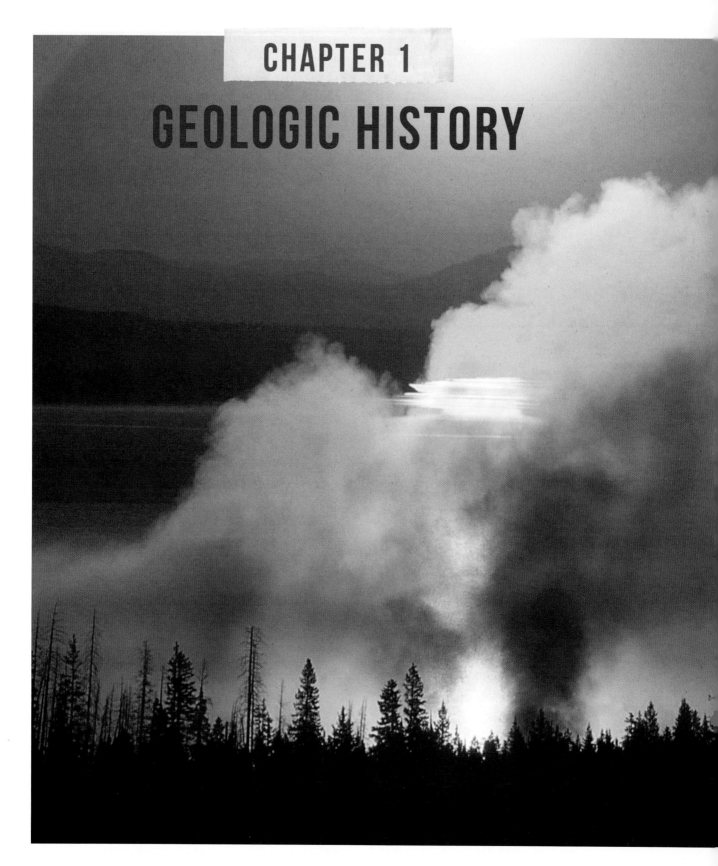

CHAPTER 1
GEOLOGIC HISTORY

Sunrise over the Potts thermal area on the west side of Yellowstone Lake. This sunrise was colored red by smoke from regional forest fires, and with some imagination the redness combined with the rising steam conjures thoughts about the explosion of the great Yellowstone caldera, a cataclysmic event that happened about 640,000 years ago. Indeed, Yellowstone Lake itself fills a portion of the

crater that did not refill with lava flows that oozed forth in the wake of the titanic eruption. Given the lake's elevation of 7,733 feet above sea level, it is remarkable that there is enough land that is higher in elevation to catch enough rain and snow to fill the lake's basin. JEFF HENRY/ROCHE JAUNE PICTURES, INC.

BY GEOLOGIC STANDARDS, MOST OF WHAT WE SEE ON THE SURFACE OF TODAY'S YELLOWSTONE IS VERY YOUNG. There are a few outcrops of what is known as the Beartooth Uplift in the northern sections of the park that expose Precambrian rock aged around 2.7 billion years, making them the oldest surface rocks in Yellowstone. By way of comparison, the Absaroka and Gallatin Mountain Ranges, which bracket the park on its east and west borders, respectively, are only in the neighborhood of 45 to 50 million years old. There are some lava flows in the park that are as young as 70,000 years. Much younger still are geothermal

Professor Eric Boyd of Montana State University draws a water sample from a hot springs runoff channel in the Norris Geyser Basin. Eric is a highly qualified researcher permitted (Permit #YELL-2018-SCI-05544) by the National Park Service in Yellowstone to perform fascinating research into thermophiles—life forms adapted to living in the scalding waters of Yellowstone's hot springs. Eric describes the work he does in Yellowstone: "These studies provide insight into environmental conditions that may have promoted the origin of life on Earth during a time of increased vulcanism and that may sustain life on other volcanically active planets."
ERIC BOYD, MONTANA STATE UNIVERSITY

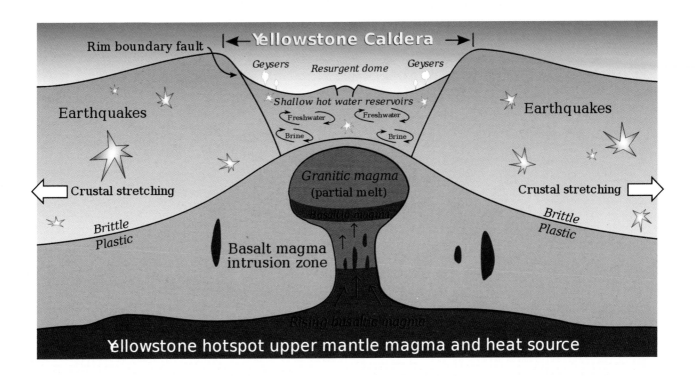

Rim boundary fault

|← **Yellowstone Caldera** →|

Geysers   *Resurgent dome*   Geysers

Earthquakes

Shallow hot water reservoirs

Freshwater   Freshwater

Brine   Brine

Earthquakes

← **Crustal stretching**

Crustal stretching →

Granitic magma (partial melt)

Basaltic magma

Brittle
Plastic

Brittle
Plastic

Basalt magma intrusion zone

Rising basaltic magma

Yellowstone hotspot upper mantle magma and heat source

This schematic diagram illustrates the basic principles at work in the Yellowstone caldera. These are the processes that have caused the repeated explosions of the caldera through time, and also are the general explanation for the heat source and water circulation systems that power Yellowstone's famous geysers, hot springs, and geothermal expressions. YELLOWSTONE NATIONAL PARK

National Park Service interpretive ranger Carolyn Loren holds a diagram of the Yellowstone caldera as part of an educational field presentation to park visitors in July 2004. JEFF HENRY/ROCHE JAUNE PICTURES, INC.

Mount Doane on the left and Mount Stevenson on the right form imposing figures in this photograph shot from the summit of Top Notch Peak. All three mountains are located in the Absaroka Range east of Yellowstone Lake, where they make up a section of the eastern rim of the Yellowstone supervolcano. The Absarokas are the eroded remnants of a massive volcanic extrusion that occurred around 50 million years ago and form a sub-range of the Rocky Mountains that runs 150 miles north to south and up to 75 miles east to west. Another element of Yellowstone's geologic history, this one relatively recent, is the concavities seen on the north-facing slopes of the mountains in this picture. Cirques, as they are called, were scoured out by glacial ice, and so are only several tens of thousands of years old. JEFF HENRY/ROCHE JAUNE PICTURES, INC.

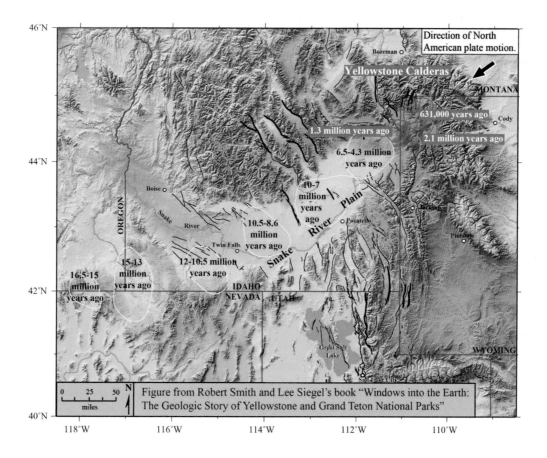

Figure from Robert Smith and Lee Siegel's book "Windows into the Earth: The Geologic Story of Yellowstone and Grand Teton National Parks"

This map by celebrated geologist and Yellowstone expert Dr. Robert Smith illustrates how the hot spot now under Yellowstone National Park has been gnawing its way through the Rocky Mountains for the last 16-plus million years. The location and date range of the various explosive events in the hot spot's history are outlined in yellow, and dates before present for the different explosions are indicated in black lettering within each of the yellow circles.

The map also clearly shows how the wide and flat Snake River Plain was left along the hot spot's path. That clear passage, and especially its southwest to northeast orientation, has had further effects on Yellowstone's geology. Because of its compass orientation, the Snake River valley has long served as a perfect conduit for storms coming from the Pacific Ocean, especially winter storms. Moisture-laden clouds from the ocean blow up the Snake River valley and are forced upward when they encounter the Yellowstone high country, which itself has been uplifted by subterranean volcanic pressure to an elevation higher than it otherwise would be. The lifting clouds then dump their moisture on Yellowstone's plateaus and mountains, a phenomenon that in glacial times accounted for the vast amounts of snowfall that morphed into glacial ice. In time these massive glaciers sculpted Yellowstone into the beautifully complex landscapes seen in the park today. YELLOWSTONE NATIONAL PARK COLLECTION

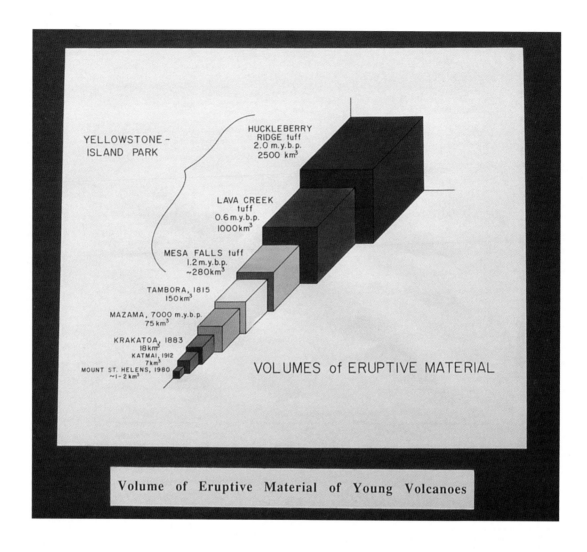

Volume of Eruptive Material of Young Volcanoes

This schematic diagram gives a relative sense of scale for various caldera explosions through history and prehistory. The Lava Creek explosion of about 640,000 years ago, the one that formed the yawning concavity that defines central Yellowstone at the present time, is the second largest depicted here. The Lava Creek eruption is dwarfed by the Huckleberry Ridge event, which was the eruption of the Yellowstone hot spot a little over 2 million years ago. Still smaller is the Mesa Falls blowup, which occurred about midway in time between Lava Creek and Huckleberry Ridge. All three of the most recent Yellowstone explosions were vastly larger than the 1980s eruption of Mount St. Helens (depicted here on the left end of the display).

YELLOWSTONE NATIONAL PARK COLLECTION

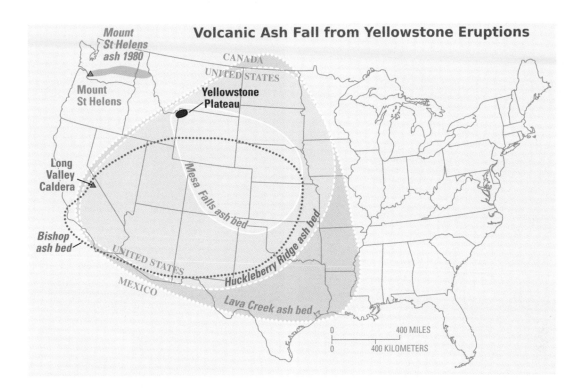

Volcanic Ash Fall from Yellowstone Eruptions

deposits, almost all of which are less than 14,000 years old, with some deposits having been laid down within the last few years.

The youngest of Yellowstone National Park's geologic macro features, and the one that is probably best known, is the great Yellowstone caldera. Most maps show the caldera's dominant presence across a large expanse of the central section of the park. Occurring only about 640,000 years ago, the volcanic blast that created the immense concavity we see today was only the latest in a series of more than one hundred similarly colossal explosions that were spaced out geographically over hundreds of miles and temporally over millions of years as the North American Plate moved southwesterly over the Yellowstone hot spot. The course of those explosions can be graphically traced along the flume-like course of

This map illustration gives some idea of the consequences of an eruption of the Yellowstone hot spot and also includes the fallout zone from other volcanic eruptions to give a sense of relative scale. The fallout field from the 1980 explosion of Mount St. Helens, for example, is shown in yellow across an expanse of Washington and Idaho. The depiction of Mount St. Helens's ash field is not exactly accurate, because I and others who were here at the time clearly recall that a small amount of ash did fall on Yellowstone, but the map nonetheless serves to illustrate that the 1980 event was vastly smaller than any of the explosions of the Yellowstone caldera. YELLOWSTONE NATIONAL PARK COLLECTION

Columnar basalt at Sheepeater Cliffs. These peculiar fencepost-like formations are found in at least three different locations in Yellowstone, as well as in other areas outside the park. They can be seen within the park on both sides of the Yellowstone River in the vicinity of the Overhanging Cliff and Calcite Springs, and also where this photograph was taken at the Sheepeater Cliffs along the Gardner River a few miles south of Mammoth Hot Springs. By geologic standards, the basalt forming these hexagonal columns is young—only about 1.3 million years old. JEFF HENRY/ROCHE JAUNE PICTURES, INC.

Bob Smith is a world-renowned geologist with a lifelong association with Yellowstone. He has family ties extending back to the earliest days of the development of the gateway town of West Yellowstone, and Bob was a young college student when he began working a summer job with the US Fish & Wildlife Service. After a few years working with fish, Bob switched his interest to geology, where one of his first research endeavors was investigating the notorious 1959 Hebgen Lake earthquake just outside Yellowstone. His distinguished career in geology helped lead to the founding of a US Geological Survey organization called the Yellowstone Volcano Observatory, where work done by Bob and his associates has revealed most of what is known about the great Yellowstone caldera. In this photograph Bob points at sensors installed to monitor volcanic activity in the park from a location near the top of Lake Butte, which is located along the eastern rim of the enormous caldera. JIM PEACO, YELLOWSTONE NATIONAL PARK COLLECTION

A rare double arch in an undisclosed location in Yellowstone National Park. Much of the rock in the Absaroka and Gallatin Mountain Ranges in Yellowstone is volcanic breccia, which is a mixture of large and small chunks of rock incorporated into a matrix of finer-grained material. The Yellowstone breccia, which is often referred to as Absaroka breccia for the dominating mountain range along the eastern boundary of the park, formed when a viscous flow of rhyolite moved so slowly that its surface had time to cool and solidify. Still-molten lava underneath the surface eventually moved and rolled the erstwhile surface into the flowing mass, cracking the solidified surface into pieces that were then mixed into the still-fluid rock below. When the flow finally came to a halt and cooled completely, the fractured chunks of rock that had formed on the surface remained, separate and identifiable within the mass. By its nature breccia is crumbly, and that erosiveness combined with the vagaries of wind, rain, snow, and ice resulted in this striking double arch deep in Yellowstone's backcountry. JEFF HENRY/ROCHE JAUNE PICTURES, INC.

National Park Service interpretive ranger Melanie Weeks Condon leads a school group past a hot springs runoff channel at Mammoth Hot Springs. Melanie has worked for many years in Yellowstone, most recently as an educational ranger with Expedition Yellowstone, a park service program through which school groups from around the nation come to Yellowstone to learn about the park's wonders. JEFF HENRY/ROCHE JAUNE PICTURES, INC.

National Aeronautics and Space Administration scientist Paul D. Sebesta collects water and mud samples from Turbid Lake. The lake fills a steam explosion crater along Sedge Creek just south of Pelican Valley. Steam explosions are thought to occur when pressure holding a lid on superheated water is removed and the water flashes to steam and violently expands. There have been countless steam explosions in Yellowstone's geologic history, with at least one occurring near Nymph Lake as recently as 2003. Most such explosions are small, spewing rocks and debris only a few feet. Turbid Lake, however, covers about 143 acres. As its names suggests, its waters are turbid with dissolved minerals, very acidic, and noticeably warm but not scalding.

Paul Sebesta was a NASA scientist in 1986 when he noticed Turbid Lake presenting an unusual powder blue color on satellite images. He came to Yellowstone to investigate, and as a young park ranger I helped him by backpacking his inflatable raft and other equipment on the four-mile hike to the lake. I then had the privilege of paddling around the lake with Paul and helping him collect samples from the shores and center of the lake. JEFF HENRY/ROCHE JAUNE PICTURES, INC.

National Geographic's Boyd Mattson and National Park Service geologist Rick Hutchinson paddle on Grand Prismatic Spring. Hutchinson had this boat specially designed for use on Yellowstone's hot springs. Rick's foremost consideration was to have the boat balanced so it could not capsize; after construction he took it to a cool-water lake and jumped up and down on its gunwales in a deliberate but unsuccessful attempt to flip it over. Rick also had a portal built in the center of the boat, through which he could access the waters of hot springs to take samples, temperatures, and so on. The boat was built with plywood laminated with glue that would not soften in high temperatures. In the end the boat worked to Rick's expectations, but unfortunately—or perhaps fittingly—it was crushed by a slab of snow sliding off a rooftop, not long after Rick's own death in an avalanche.

Boyd Mattson was the host for television's *National Geographic Explorer* from 1995 through 2003. He was filming an episode on Yellowstone for the series when this photograph was shot in the middle of Grand Prismatic Spring in July 1995. JEFF HENRY/ROCHE JAUNE PICTURES, INC.

National Park Service interpretive ranger Tiffany Potter uses a long fishing pole to dip a thermometer into Churning Cauldron in the Mud Volcano area. Tiffany was an interpretive ranger from the late 1990s into the early 2000s and participated in a National Park Service program to monitor thermal activity in the Mud Volcano complex, which, even by the standards of Yellowstone's geothermal basins, is extremely volatile. Churning Cauldron itself was a cool-water spring until earthquakes in 1978 and 1979 morphed it into what it is today—a churning cauldron of hot, highly acidic water. JEFF HENRY/ROCHE JAUNE PICTURES, INC.

the Snake River Plain west of Yellowstone Park. It is, of course, the Yellowstone hot spot that fuels the park's famous hot springs and other geothermal expressions, which is also the inspiration for many television shows that sensationalize the catastrophic consequences of the next explosion. As several of the illustrations on the following pages show, the results of the next explosion indeed will be dire, if and when it occurs, but there are currently a number of scientific monitoring programs in place that presumably would give some warning before the event.

The last explosion of the Yellowstone caldera blew out roughly 240 cubic miles of material, or about 1,000 times the volume of Mount Saint Helens's 1980 eruption. Following the explosion were profuse lava and ash flows that partially filled the cavity left by the blast. There were also subsequent smaller explosions, such as the one about

Cave Falls on the Bechler River viewed from inside its namesake cave. Waterfalls are common in the Bechler region in the southwestern corner of the park. Most streams there head in the higher plateau country to the north, toward the center of Yellowstone National Park. From there they flow south and west, directions that take them over successive drop-offs marking the toes of various lava flows that have occurred in Yellowstone's geologic history. The phenomenon of falling water led to the nickname for this portion of Yellowstone National Park—Cascade Corner—and also accounts for an early-day name for the Bechler River, the Falling Fork, a name that dates to the romantic days of the Rocky Mountain fur trade of the beginning decades of the nineteenth century. In an example of ongoing geologic processes, the cave for which this twenty-foot-high waterfall was named has collapsed, so it is no longer possible to duplicate this photograph. JEFF HENRY/ROCHE JAUNE PICTURES, INC.

National Park Service soil scientist Ann Rodman inspects a sample excavated from a backcountry test pit in the Gallatin Mountain Range. Ann was in charge of a parkwide soil survey in Yellowstone in the 1990s. When this photo was taken in August 1993, she was in the middle of a weeklong trek through the northwestern part of the park, carrying a shovel and digging numerous test pits along the way, then packing out an impressive load of soil samples from the many excavations she made on the trip. JEFF HENRY/ROCHE JAUNE PICTURES, INC.

174,000 years ago that created the West Thumb of Yellowstone Lake. And several times since the last great caldera explosion, the region has been scoured by stupendous glaciers, the most recent of which is referred to as the Pinedale glaciation. The Pinedale commenced about 115,000 years ago, and the Yellowstone Plateau did not entirely melt free of its glacial ice until about 14,000 years ago. It's almost as hard to envision the amount of ice that was present in Yellowstone—figuratively speaking until just yesterday—as it is to conceive of the magnitude and power of the caldera explosion. The huge ice cap covered nearly all of today's park and extended out and over the surrounding mountains for a long distance in all directions, while rivers of ice flowed down valleys leading away from the mountains. The ice cap was centered on Yellowstone Lake, where the icy mantle was between 3,000 and 4,000 feet thick. The pressure and movement of such enormous amounts of ice acted as coarse sandpaper and shaped the

National Park Service geologist Rick Hutchinson cleans litter from Morning Glory Pool in 1991. Rick Hutchinson was a dedicated scientist who lived and worked in Yellowstone from the early 1970s until his untimely death in an avalanche near Heart Lake in March 1997. He was a friendly, helpful man who was also a walking encyclopedia of information about Yellowstone's geothermal features, and his death was a great loss both to science and to the Yellowstone community. Here he is pictured with main-tenance workers who had pumped down the level of Morning Glory Pool so Rick could use a long-handled implement to remove debris thought-lessly thrown into the hot spring by park visitors. Some sources claim that such abuse has caused Morning Glory's famed blue color to fade since it was originally named. JEFF HENRY/ ROCHE JAUNE PICTURES, INC.

This massive petrified tree stump in the Gallatin Petrified Forest was a living redwood until it was buried in a volcanic eruption about 50 million years ago. There are at least twenty-seven distinct layers of petrified trees in Yellowstone, each buried by a separate eruption. Remarkably, this indicates to geologists that the intervals between eruptions were long enough for erupted materials not only to cool but also to degrade into soil capable of supporting a mature forest. In addition to petrified redwoods, geologists have identified other trees that are foreign to the Yellowstone region today, including sycamores, oaks, magnolias, and maples. The redwood stump pictured here is particularly large, measuring twenty-seven feet, ten inches in circumference. The stump dwarfs Colin Brooks of Bristol, England, standing on its uphill side. JEFF HENRY/ROCHE JAUNE PICTURES, INC.

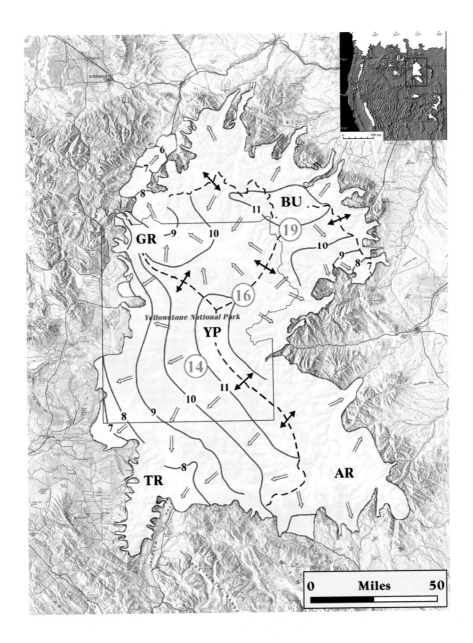

This depiction of the colossal Pinedale Glacier as it sat atop what is now Yellowstone National Park was compiled by accomplished geologists Dr. Ken Pierce and Dr. Joseph Licciardi. The Pinedale glaciation is considered to have lasted from about 30,000 to 11,700 years ago. The map shows the ice at its greatest extent, a state known to glaciologists as the glacial maximum, which is outlined as the white expanse extending beyond Yellowstone Park's borders. Black letters abbreviate key geographical points: BU for Beartooth Uplift, GR for Gallatin Range, YP for Yellowstone Plateau, TR for Teton Range, and AR for Absaroka Range. The blue contour lines mark the surface elevation of the glacial ice, which generally was 1,000 to 4,000 feet thick. Green numbers indicate the extent of glacial meltback in thousands of years before the present. Black hash lines mark the dividing ridges in the glacial mass, while black directional arrows spanning mountain divides indicate contrasting directional flows away from the icy crests.

When standing anywhere in Yellowstone, say on the shores of Yellowstone Lake, it is mind-numbing to ponder so much ice and consider that only a short geologic time ago, the ice at that spot was well over 3,000 feet thick. That amount of ice would amount to a force of over 200,000 pounds of pressure per square foot of surface area on the land beneath it. KEN PIERCE AND JOSEPH LICCIARDI

This view of Yellowstone's famous Lamar Valley was shot from a vantage west of the crossing of the Lamar River known as Buffalo Ford, which in turn is about a mile upstream from Junction Butte. Lamar Valley was heavily impacted by the most recent round of glaciation, known regionally as the Pinedale glaciation. The lumpy knolls in the middle distance of this photograph, as well as the kettle ponds that dot the valley, are all evidence of a huge glacier that filled the valley just a wink of geologic time ago.

The rocks that form the foundation of Yellowstone were laid down in some cases hundreds of millions of years ago. After formation the rocks were subjected to all manner of twisting, heaving, compressing, and contorting forces. They were also exposed to the ongoing effects of erosion, and about 640,000 years ago were impacted by the cataclysmic explosion of the Yellowstone caldera. It was the ice of the Pinedale period that served as a polishing event to put a finish on the splendid landscapes we see in the park today. JEFF HENRY/ROCHE JAUNE PICTURES, INC.

landscape of today's Yellowstone, and the erosive processes of wind, water, and gravity that followed the disappearance of the ice acted as fine sandpaper to put the finishing touches on the park's present appearance.

Geologically, the most immediately dramatic expressions in Yellowstone are the park's famous geysers, hot springs, mudpots, and fumeroles, most of which are located within the boundaries of the caldera. In the context of cultural history, they are the most important geologic elements, too, because it was their existence, along with the Grand Canyon of the Yellowstone River, that inspired the establishment of Yellowstone as a park in 1872. In Yellowstone it is often said that geology drives biology. A moment's thought reveals that dictum to be true everywhere, but its truth is especially apparent here, where a mostly intact ecosystem with a healthy contingent of wildlife exists primarily because of the protections that come with Yellowstone's status as a national park. Without its geologic history there would be no Yellowstone National Park, and neither would its famed wildlife exist in the numbers and variety we see today.

CHAPTER 2
NATIVE AMERICANS

Photo of rock art at undisclosed location just east of Yellowstone National Park. This example of Native American rock art is typical of a style common in the Yellowstone area. Although no prehistoric rock art is known to exist within the boundaries of modern Yellowstone, its absence may be due to the fact that there is little to no rock suitable as a surface for engraving or painting inside the park. Rock art not far outside the park is common, however, and the style of much of that art

has been linked to tribes known to have ranged within the area that was designated Yellowstone National Park on March 1, 1872.

Vandalism of irreplaceable rock art is a chronic problem. Several bullet holes scarring this panel of prehistoric art can be seen in the photo. JEFF HENRY/ROCHE JAUNE PICTURES, INC.

THIRTEEN THOUSAND YEARS—THAT'S THE MINIMUM amount of time that Native Americans have been in the Yellowstone area, which means they arrived not long after the ice of the last glaciation period had melted away. That also means they were here for about sixty-five times the length of time that Euro-Americans have been, and more than eighty-five times as long as Yellowstone has existed as a park. We know this time frame to be accurate because projectile points dated to the Clovis culture and wrought from Yellowstone obsidian have been found in the area, and the origin of the Clovis culture has been established by archaeologists at about 13,200 calendar years before the present.

Successive cultures evolved in the Yellowstone area after the Clovis, each one identifiable by its distinctive types of stone projectile points and tools. Notably, Yellowstone obsidian is represented in the tool assemblages of all these cultures, particularly at archaeological sites in the region surrounding the park. But Yellowstone obsidian, especially that from the park's famous Obsidian Cliff, was so highly valued by indigenous peoples that artifacts fashioned from it have been found as far north as Canada, as far south as extreme southern Kansas, and as far east as central Ohio. Inhabitants

Prehistoric Man with Atlatl is a painting by Wyoming artist James Bama. The atlatl, or spear thrower, was an ingenious invention made at least 30,000 years ago. Effectively it acts as a lever for someone throwing a spear, greatly increasing power and range in a manner similar to the way a lacrosse stick does for someone throwing a lacrosse ball. The atlatl lever can be seen here in the man's right hand, and a closer look reveals the small peg on the end of the atlatl that fits into a corresponding socket on the end of the atlatl dart, which generally was smaller than a thrusting spear. There is evidence that atlatls and darts were used by prehistoric residents of the Yellowstone Park area from the very earliest times, at least 13,000 years ago. JAMES AND LYNNE BAMA, USED WITH PERMISSION

The incomparable Western artist James Bama rendered this painting of a young Native American woman grinding sage while kneeling on a buffalo robe, titled *Sage Grinder*. The rounded stone the woman is holding in her hands is known as a *mano*, which is Spanish for "hand." The larger, flat stone is known as a *metate*, a word derived from the Central American Indian word *metatl*, which roughly means "grinding stone." Paired together the mano and metate served to grind not only sage for ceremonial purposes, but also dried foods from both plants and animals. The ovate metate the woman is using in this painting is a type that was common in the Yellowstone region.

James Bama has spent almost sixty years of his life in the Cody, Wyoming, area, and so most of his extraordinary body of work has been focused on the Yellowstone region. Jim's wife, Lynne, is an accomplished writer. JAMES AND LYNNE BAMA, USED WITH PERMISSION

This prehistoric firepit was photographed by the author in 1999. It was one of several such hearths in the immediate area that had been uncovered by natural processes of erosion, possibly when large plates of fractured ice blew in from Yellowstone Lake and gouged the bank as the lake thawed during the previous spring. Whatever the erosional cause, the firepits were beautifully exposed, like the seeds in the center of an apple that had been deftly cut in half. JEFF HENRY/ROCHE JAUNE PICTURES, INC.

The elevated profile of this dam structure built at right angles across the streambed of Tangled Creek to form Ranger Pool can be seen extending from the foreground to the opposite bank of the stream beyond the tuft of tawny vegetation. As late as the mid-twentieth century, before they were plastered over with accreted silica deposits, log ends could be seen sticking out of the structure, a strong indication that the logs had been placed across the creek by human hands. Given the slow rate of deposition of the silica-based rock dissolved in the waters of Tangled Creek, most experts conclude that the dam had been constructed before the arrival of Euro-Americans in the Yellowstone area, and indeed the ethnographic record offers abundant evidence that there was strong affinity for warm geothermal water by the Native Americans who inhabited the Yellowstone region.

Ranger Pool had a long history of use as a swimming pool by park employees during the late nineteenth and early twentieth centuries, an activity that has been illegal for most of Yellowstone Park's history and strictly enforced in today's park. Naturally, Native Americans liked to soak in warm water as much as anybody else, and doing so was perfectly acceptable in the days before Yellowstone was established as a park and human use of the area was much less intense. JEFF HENRY/ROCHE JAUNE PICTURES, INC.

---

continued to use Yellowstone obsidian for their tools and weapons right up until the time of contact with Euro-Americans in the eighteenth and nineteenth centuries, leaving no doubt that they not only had intimate knowledge of the Yellowstone area and its resources, but also were connected to trade or travel networks on a nearly continental scale.

That Yellowstone was known and used by Native Americans is also evidenced by the abundance of prehistoric campsites in what is now the park. These peoples were like any others with regard to selecting camping spots: They looked for sites near water that also provided fuel, food sources, and shelter, as well as level spots on which to sleep and engage in everyday activities. Sites along watercourses and lakeshores were preferred. Those predilections are reflected in the archaeological record, where many sites with favorable characteristics have signs of more or less continuous use through thousands of years of occupancy. The Fishing Bridge area is a prime example—the site is level, with inexhaustible water supplies, and

These two exquisite artifacts are from the Clovis culture period, which evolved in North America around 13,000 years ago. They were found as part of an extraordinary deposit of more than 115 artifacts that had been buried with a male child aged one to two years at death. The boy's skeleton and the stash of artifacts were accidentally discovered in 1968 in a cavern along the Shields River near Wilsall, Montana. The Anzick Site, named for the family owning the land where the discovery was made, is a little less than seventy straight-line miles north of Yellowstone National Park. Along with surface discoveries of a few Clovis artifacts scattered within the boundaries of the present park, the Anzick Site makes clear that members of the Clovis culture were present in the Yellowstone area, which in turn proves that ancestors of today's Native Americans have been living here for more than 13,000 years. It is sobering to think about the passage of so much time, at least in the context of human existence. To put it in perspective, the Anzick toddler and his contingent of Clovis artifacts had been buried in their concavity on the banks of the Shields River for well over 8,000 years before construction of the Great Pyramid of Giza even began. JEFF HENRY/ROCHE JAUNE PICTURES, INC.

This fragment of a Clovis point was found during a construction project about two blocks outside Yellowstone in Gardiner, Montana, the town situated at the park's North Entrance. The whereabouts of the point today is unknown and it has therefore been lost to science, but it is known that it was made from obsidian. The likelihood is that the obsidian was sourced from Obsidian Cliff, so the artifact is yet another strong indication that Clovis peoples were active in the Yellowstone area and had detailed knowledge of the lands that came to be designated as the national park in 1872. LARRY LAHREN/ANTHRO RESEARCH COLLECTION, USED WITH PERMISSION

it was undoubtedly a good place to fish, hunt, and find natural plant foods. It was also situated along natural travel routes up and down the Yellowstone River and around Yellowstone Lake, and indeed the evidence shows that prehistoric peoples used the area intensively for a very long time.

The ethnographic record also proves that Native Americans in the region around Yellowstone knew the area that became the park very well. As early as the 1790s there are indications that tribes from as far away as what is now North Dakota provided accurate information about the ultimate source of the Yellowstone River—which is actually south of today's park—to David Thompson, the great Canadian explorer and cartographer. In 1805 those same people gave Lewis and Clark another tantalizing detail about the

Self-taken photo of the author with wickiup in an undisclosed location within Yellowstone National Park. These relics of the past remind us that the past in Yellowstone is really not that distant at all. On the other hand, it is also remarkable that these structures managed to weather Yellowstone's severe climate as long as they did, standing for decades as reminders of the Native Americans who lived here before the park was created. All the wickiups found in Yellowstone must have been constructed before about 1880, but now, more than 140 years later, almost all have finally succumbed to the forces of weather and gravity and have fallen to the ground.
JEFF HENRY/ROCHE JAUNE PICTURES, INC.

Yellowstone River when they related that there was "a considerable fall" on the river somewhere within the mountains, an almost certain reference to what we know today as the Grand Canyon of the Yellowstone and its Upper and Lower Falls; Native nations in what is now North Dakota also related to the Lewis and Clark Corps of Discovery that "a good road passes up this river [the Yellowstone] to its extreme source." In the years after Lewis and Clark, American Indians served as guides to fur trappers and other Euro-Americans. A group of Pend d'Oreilles, for example, guided mountain man Warren Angus Ferris to the geyser basins along the Firehole

For most of the nineteenth century the Yellowstone area was on the northeastern fringe of the Bannock tribe's range, but the area that became the park was well known and used by the tribe. The Bannocks were culturally affiliated with the Northern Shoshone tribe, who perhaps are somewhat better known than the Bannocks, and today both live on the Fort Hall Reservation, located on a small sliver of their former lands along the Snake River about twenty miles northeast of the city of Pocatello, Idaho. WILLIAM HENRY JACKSON, YELLOWSTONE NATIONAL PARK COLLECTION

Photograph by Edward Sheriff Curtis of two Crow men on horseback in falling snow. In the years leading up to and including Yellowstone's creation as a park in 1872, the Crows lived mostly along the lower Yellowstone River and its tributaries to the east of the area that became the park. They nonetheless often ranged into what is now Yellowstone National Park, and they knew the area intimately. After the park was created, Crows were often invited by the park's bureaucracy to visit Yellowstone, usually to participate in some sort of ceremony. At various times they attended seasonal openings of the park's gates, and on several occasions during the 1920s they were brought in to participate in staged buffalo stampedes in Lamar Valley. At least two of these stampedes were filmed as part of a Hollywood production titled *The Thundering Herd*, a movie that had two iterations, one in 1925 and the other in 1933.

Edward Sheriff Curtis (1868–1952) was a photographer and ethnographer who devoted much of his long life to documenting American Indians, mostly in the western United States, during a time when they still retained some semblance of their culture prior to contact with Euro-Americans. LIBRARY OF CONGRESS

This well-composed painting by West Yellowstone, Montana, artist Mike Bryers shows three Native Americans quarrying obsidian near the rim of Yellowstone's iconic Obsidian Cliff, while the pair in the foreground engage in what archaeologists refer to as "reduction work." Reduction work was just that—chipping away unwanted material to lighten the load of stone that had to be carried from quarries back to camp.

Obsidian from Obsidian Cliff furnished extremely high-quality material for prehistoric peoples to use in the manufacture of tools and weapons. It is the dominant lithic material found in archaeological sites in the immediate area around Yellowstone and for long distances in all directions. Native Americans found Yellowstone obsidian so easy to work and so effective as tools and projectile points that the material was traded or otherwise transported across vast areas of North America—obsidian originating in Yellowstone has been found in archaeological sites at least as far away as southern Kansas and south-central Ohio. So sharp are the fractured edges of this volcanic glass that modern-day archaeologists who have found themselves in need of surgical procedures have furnished knives made of obsidian to their surgeons, and indeed obsidian knives can be sharpened to an edge much more keen than the edge of surgical instruments made of metal. MIKE BRYERS, USED WITH PERMISSION

These beautiful artifacts, created by a highly skilled artisan almost 2,000 years ago, were excavated from earthen burial mounds in the Scioto River valley at Hopewell Culture National Historical Park near Chillicothe, Ohio. They were wrought from obsidian that has been chemically identified as originating from Obsidian Cliff in today's Yellowstone National Park. Microscopic examination of the shiny black blades further revealed no sign of utilitarian wear, so the objects were almost certainly used for ceremony and symbolism only. Hundreds of such artifacts, along with hundreds of pounds of unworked obsidian, have been unearthed at Hopewell. Exactly how so much obsidian made the 1,400-mile straight-line journey from Obsidian Cliff to the Hopewell burial mounds is not clear. Perhaps some individuals from what is now Ohio made the entire trip to present-day Yellowstone Park, or perhaps someone or a group of people from today's Wyoming made the trip all the way to Ohio with a load of obsidian. More likely the volcanic glass was shuttled along a network of traders that extended from the Rocky Mountains to the Scioto River valley, but it is almost certain that we will never know for sure. ANDREW W. WEILAND/HOPEWELL CULTURE NATIONAL HISTORICAL PARK, USED WITH PERMISSION

River in 1834 on what is often described as the first tourist excursion to Yellowstone, because Ferris's objective was to see the geothermal wonders of the area rather than pursue economic interests.

In 1865, a missionary named Father Francis Xavier Kuppens was living with the Blackfeet near the site of today's Great Falls, Montana, when he heard stories from them about the geysers and hot springs around the heads of the Madison and Yellowstone Rivers. When asked by the missionary, the Blackfeet readily consented to guide him to the area of the future park and exhibited detailed knowledge about the

In this photograph (top), probably taken in 1871 by pioneer photographer William Henry Jackson in the Yellowstone River valley north of today's park, a Nez Perce woman has spread out strips of meat to dry on what looks to be a bison hide. The Nez Perce lived west of Yellowstone, primarily in today's central Idaho and eastern Washington and Oregon. Early in the nineteenth century they hunted bison on the Snake River Plain close to their homeland, but by 1840 those herds had been overhunted by Euro-American hunters, and also by Native Americans to supply hides to traders in return for manufactured goods. After that date the Nez Perce and other tribes living in the North-west had to cross the Continental Divide to hunt the bison that were still numerous on the Great Plains east of the Rocky Mountains. Likely the Nez Perce group to which this woman belonged had crossed over the mountains to the plains, hunters in her village had been successful, and, as was the custom, the women cut up the slain animals and processed the meat. The pattern of western tribes migrating over the mountains to hunt buffalo was short-lived, however—by the late 1870s the US government had more strictly confined Native Americans to their reservations, and by the early 1880s the big herds of buffalo on the Great Plains had disappeared. WILLIAM HENRY JACKSON, YELLOWSTONE NATIONAL PARK COLLECTION

This photograph (bottom) was almost certainly taken at the same time and place as the one of the Nez Perce woman spreading out strips of meat to dry. It is simply a wider overview of the same camp, which was probably located near the Crow Agency on Mission Creek just east of today's Livingston, Montana. Photographer William Henry Jackson is known to have stopped by the agency on Mission Creek on the same trip that took him to what was to become Yellowstone National Park with the Hayden Survey of 1871. WILLIAM HENRY JACKSON, YELLOWSTONE NATIONAL PARK COLLECTION

---

area when they arrived—this despite the fact that the home range of the Blackfeet was considerably north of Yellowstone, primarily in what is today northwestern Montana and southern Alberta. In still later years of the nineteenth century, members of the Shoshone, Bannock, Nez Perce, and other tribes are recorded as traveling through what is now Yellowstone National Park, often serving as guides to official explorers and other Euro-American travelers. In almost all recorded cases, the Native American people exhibited both broadscale and finely detailed knowledge of the area.

This evidence refutes the assertion made in the early days of Yellowstone National Park that American Indians rarely came here because they were superstitiously afraid of the area's thermal features. There are some records in early-day journals, almost certainly based on misinterpretations by Euro-American chroniclers of statements made to them by Native Americans, that may have been the original source for this misconception. Capt. William Clark, for example, made a notation on an 1808 sketch map (which contributed to his 1810 master map of the West) that is a tantalizing early-day

Through the early decades of the 1800s, sizable herds of bison lived on the Snake River Plain west of Yellowstone. Mountain man Osborne Russell wrote about the area in his journal in November 1840: "In the year 1836 large bands of Buffaloe could be seen in almost every little Valley. . . . at this time the only traces which can be seen of them were the scattered bones of those that had been killed." Still in need of the bounty that bison provided, Native Americans residing in the area of the Snake River began traveling over the Continental Divide to the great buffalo ranges east of the mountains to hunt the shaggy beasts. One of their principal routes was through what is now Yellowstone National Park on what came to be known as the Bannock Trail. The trail received heavy use for about forty years, until the Native Americans were firmly penned up on their reservations and the huge bison herds on the Great Plains had been extirpated. Evidence of that heavy use was visible in this 1955 photo with longtime park ranger David Condon, and ruts of the Bannock Trail can still be seen today in some places where the route passed through the park. YELLOWSTONE NATIONAL PARK COLLECTION

reference to the park area, although misleading as to how Native Americans probably felt about the area's features. With his usual creative spelling and capitalization, Clark wrote, "At the head of this river [the Yellowstone] the natives give an account that there is frequently herd [sic] a loud noise, like Thunder, which makes the earth Tremble, they State they seldom go there because their children cannot sleep—and conceive it possessed of spirits, who were averse that men should be near them." On Warren Angus Ferris's 1834 trip to see the geothermal displays of the Firehole Valley, he wrote that his Native American guides were "appalled" by being close to hot springs

Photo of Native American–built enclosure of rocks in an undisclosed location in northern Yellowstone National Park. This circle, possibly a vision quest site, faces east toward the rising sun on an open hilltop south of Mammoth Hot Springs. Native Americans worshipped the sun and often built such enclosures and sat within them, often for days at a time, waiting for a vision that would lend them power for their journey through life. The vision and the power-giver usually came in the form of a spirit animal, which would confer some of its strength and wisdom to the supplicant. Often viewed in modern times as happening after the individual had suffered hunger or thirst to the point of hallucination, the grueling endeavor of vision questing might alternatively be seen as an act of self-sacrifice to a higher being, as an offering of respect in return for the granting of power and wisdom. Such self-sacrifice in the pursuit of a religious endeavor is not unique to Native American cultures. JEFF HENRY/ ROCHE JAUNE PICTURES, INC.

Mariah Gale Henry stands inside a prehistoric observation blind overlooking Paradise Valley just north of Yellowstone National Park. The site of this enclosure of rocks offers a splendid view and may have been used to screen the observer from game or enemies in the valley below. The ponds in the middle distance of this photograph are artificial creations of much more recent vintage, while the Yellowstone River may be seen curling along the right side of the frame. The crest of the high, snowy ridge in the far background marks the northwestern boundary of Yellowstone National Park. JEFF HENRY/ROCHE JAUNE PICTURES, INC.

This stone structure on the north shore of Yellowstone Lake at Bridge Bay is submerged during the high water of early summer, so it's best to seek it out for viewing or a photograph later in the year. Reputed to be a Native American fish trap, authorities seem to be equally divided as to whether the rock alignment actually was constructed by Native Americans and used to catch fish. A point that seems pertinent to me is that before lake trout appeared in Yellowstone Lake in the mid-1990s, native cutthroat trout spent early summer in relatively shallow portions of the lake and then retreated to deeper water in late summer. The cutthroat would only be available in the shallow water within the perimeter of this structure during early summer, which was when thousands upon thousands of the trout were readily available to American Indians in the numerous spawning streams around the lake. It would not have been energetically efficient for them to invest the effort required to build this rock formation when they could have easily scooped fish out of spawning streams with their bare hands at the same time of year. One theory on how the supposed fish trap came to be is that the rocks were "bulldozed" into their linear arrangement by the wind blowing large plates of fractured ice across the lake during spring thaw. JEFF HENRY/ROCHE JAUNE PICTURES, INC.

and geysers, "congratulated" him on his supposed narrow escape after he returned from a closer view of the springs, and remarked that "hell, which they had heard about from the whites, must be in the vicinity."

It is far more probable that Clark, Ferris, and others misunderstood what their Native American informants were trying to tell them, rather than that they were actually afraid of Yellowstone's geothermals to the point that they never or rarely ventured into the area. As argued above, there is overwhelming evidence that American Indians not only visited the area that later became the park, but were extremely familiar with it. It is much more likely that they were trying to explain to the early-day explorers of the region that the hot springs and geyser areas had special spiritual powers, and that those spirits needed to be appeased by any humans who intended to visit the places where the spirits resided.

What is even more likely is that the myth that Native Americans were afraid of and avoided the Yellowstone area originated in the early days of Yellowstone's existence as a park, and was created by boosters trying to attract visitors to the new reserve by allaying any fears prospective tourists might have had regarding American Indians. In this regard it is important to remember that when Yellowstone National Park was established in 1872, there were still large numbers of Native Americans living in more or less traditional ways in the West—it was, indeed, still four years until George Armstrong Custer's defeat at the Little Bighorn. Beyond the Custer debacle there was the 1877 flight of the Nez Perce through the five-year-old park, and another similar but lesser-known flight of Bannocks through the park in 1878. There followed still more years of frequent "scares" in the Yellowstone region that were mostly exaggerated, but unfounded though they might have been, park boosters feared that such scares might dissuade would-be tourists considering a trip to the novel park. It was important to early-day park advocates to neutralize those fears and attract tourists as a way of ensuring the park's continued existence, and so in their minds it behooved them to create and then perpetuate the absurdity that Native Americans had always been and continued to be fearful of and absent from the area.

Because of Yellowstone's notoriously ferocious winters, it is clear that at the time of Euro-American contact most Native Americans visited the Yellowstone Plateau only in the summer and fall. Given the fact that they and their ancestors had been in the Yellowstone area for at least 13,000 years by the time Euro-Americans showed up, and that the climate of the area changed substantially several times over the course of those millennia, it is possible that at some points during all that time, settlement and use of the Yellowstone plateau might have been different. Especially during eras when the climate was warmer and dryer, specifically during the so-called Altithermal period

Washakie was a great warrior and leader of the branch of the Shoshone tribe that lived in the Yellowstone area. He is pictured front and center of a group of his people with a manufactured hat in his right hand, while in his left he holds an object that is not completely identifiable but may be a medicine bundle. If so, it would be fitting, as the contrast between the cowboy-like hat in one hand and a magical talisman in the other would be symbolic of Washakie's life. Some sources report that he was born as early as 1798 and did not even see a Euro-American until 1811. The decades of his life passed through the eras of fur trappers, gold prospectors, and official explorers, and ultimately to the period of Euro-American settlement of the Shoshones' homeland with its concomitant development of roads, telegraph lines, railroads, agriculture, cities, and the restriction of Washakie's people to reservations. By the time Washakie died at more than one hundred years of age on February 20, 1900, Wyoming had been a state for almost ten years, and it had been almost twenty-eight years since Yellowstone had been established as a park. As with most free-ranging Native Americans of his time, Washakie had an in-depth knowledge of a vast amount of territory, including the land that was designated the world's first national park. YELLOWSTONE NATIONAL PARK COLLECTION

Steatite is a white soapstone, soft and relatively easy to carve in its native state, but readily blackened and hardened in fire after artisans sculpted it into useful forms. Capt. Meriwether Lewis noted on August 23, 1805, while observing a group of Shoshones just west of today's park, that "their culinary eutensils [*sic*] . . . consist of pots in the form of a jar made of . . . a white soft stone which becomes black and very hard by birning [*sic*] . . ." The five steatite vessels in this photograph were recovered by archaeologists in the Yellowstone region and are presently on display in the Dubois Museum and Wind River Historical Center in Dubois, Wyoming, a little over one hundred miles southeast of Yellowstone National Park. STEFANIE KOWALSZYK/DUBOIS MUSEUM AND WIND RIVER HISTORICAL CENTER, USED WITH PERMISSION

of about 5,000 to 9,000 years ago, it is believable that the Yellowstone high country saw an increased level of year-round use. Some sources assert that lower elevations of the West, especially the plains country, might have been so hot and dry during the Altithermal that they were all but uninhabitable. Higher, cooler, and moister habitats like the Yellowstone plateau might have been much more hospitable for year-round use during that time than they were at the time of contact.

At the time of contact, it appears that the only American Indians living year-round in the park's high country were a band of Shoshones known as the Sheepeaters, named for their dietary preference for bighorn sheep. In his classic book *Journal of a Trapper*, mountain man Osborne Russell left illuminating accounts of the Sheepeaters based on several meetings he had with them in the Yellowstone area in the 1830s. One meeting in particular, in what we today call Lamar Valley, moved Russell to leave a detailed

These National Park Service archaeologists are shown at work at a bison kill site on the shores of Yellowstone Lake on June 30, 1994. One can be seen waist deep in the excavated pit behind the first two, while the man in the foreground is dumping a bucket of dirt from the pit into a sifting screen. The screen will then be used to sift soil away from telltale artifacts. It is almost miraculous to watch breathtaking artifacts appear as if by magic from the dirt that has concealed them for long, long periods of time. JEFF HENRY/ROCHE JAUNE PICTURES, INC.

Famed Yellowstone historian Lee Whittlesey (left) and longtime Yellowstone employee and fan Tom Carter in a vision quest enclosure on top of a peak in the Gallatin Range. After a long climb these two avid hikers were enjoying the splendid view from the top of this 10,000-plus-foot peak. Others, in prehistoric times, had been similarly taken by the nature of this vantage point and had built this circular enclosure of rocks. The builders of the enclosure no doubt spent time within it, just as these two Yellowstone aficionados were doing when the picture was snapped in 1998. JEFF HENRY/ROCHE JAUNE PICTURES, INC.

description of one Sheepeater group's social composition, as well as equally detailed descriptions of their material possessions. The Sheepeaters, like all other tribes in the American West, were forced out of Yellowstone and onto reservations in the 1870s and 1880s.

For the next fifty years or so, tribes in the Yellowstone region (and elsewhere) were strictly confined to their reservations. In the 1920s, some tribe members were brought back to Yellowstone by the park's bureaucracy for special occasions, such as gate openings in the spring. It is fair to say that they were used on such occasions for the sake of spectacle to promote the park. "Spectacle" is definitely the word best used to describe the appearance of some Crows who were brought to the park to participate in the filming of a Hollywood movie on several occasions in the mid-1920s, when buffalo stampedes were staged in Lamar Valley for the benefit of a production titled *The Thundering Herd*. Native Americans put on display for the sake of show in situations like seasonal openings and Hollywood movies served to demonstrate that any danger they ever posed had been more than neutralized, and in many ways such demonstrations were similar to the way that once dangerous predators like wolves and bears had likewise been rendered harmless. Wolves were exterminated from the park, while bears were turned into garbage-eating and roadside-begging buffoons. American Indians, wolves, bears—once they all embodied images that included a component of danger, but those images were refashioned by Yellowstone promoters into new ones in which tourists could experience a bit of a thrill without risk.

Park managers in more recent times have made attempts to bring Native Americans into Yellowstone for more high-minded purposes. Kiowas, for example, recently were invited to explain their tribal creation stories, which involve thermal features in the Mud Volcano area. On another occasion Shoshones came to the park to recall ancestral memories of their forebears collecting red and orange minerals for paint in a thermal area in Pelican Valley appropriately named Vermilion Springs. Other tribes, including elements of the Sioux, have come to Yellowstone to conduct ceremonies aimed at placating the spirits of bison slaughtered by livestock interests in Montana when the animals try to migrate out of the park to escape especially hard winters in the park's interior.

The story of Native Americans in Yellowstone is long.

CHAPTER 3
EARLY EXPLORERS AND MOUNTAIN MEN

The setting of this 1871 scene by Thomas Moran is very similar to that of the following J. K. Ralston painting of Captain William Clark and his party passing through the site of present-day Livingston, Montana, on July 15, 1806. Both paintings show the gap in the mountains where the Yellowstone River flows north just before it makes its great bend to the east. Although the location in both paintings is about forty miles north of Yellowstone National Park, there is a great deal of history related to the park in the scene. The snowcapped mountain to the left is Livingston Peak. Windham Thomas Windham Quin, Earl of Dunraven, was a wealthy Scot who came to Yellowstone in 1874, just two years after the park's creation. On his way to the park, the earl noted in *The Great Divide*,

the book he wrote about his trip, that the Crows often built signal fires on the peak's summit. The canyon through which the Yellowstone flows, in the right background, was known to mountain men and many who followed as the First Canyon of the Yellowstone, and it offered one of the more geographically sensible ways to approach the country that became the park. The snow-topped Absaroka Range that runs across the skyline of the entire painting was described by Captain Clark as "a high rugged mountain" covered with "eternal snow." Snow did persist on those peaks through the summer in Clark's time and until relatively recently, but today it melts completely away almost every summer. THOMAS MORAN, GILCREASE MUSEUM, TULSA, OKLAHOMA

FAMED EXPLORERS MERIWETHER LEWIS AND WILLIAM CLARK and their Corps of Discovery were the first Americans of European descent to cross the greater Yellowstone region, but they did not enter the area encompassed by the present-day park. As a matter of fact, the closest any of them came was when Captain Clark led a portion of the party through the site of today's Livingston, Montana, on July 15, 1806. Clark's journal entries that day include a good description of the segment of the Yellowstone River that flows out of the mountains near Livingston about fifty miles north of the North Entrance to Yellowstone National Park, but they reveal no hint that he knew anything about the unusual characteristics of the headwaters of the river he called the Roche Jaune.

Bama '86
Bama A.P. 1/60

CLARK ON THE YELLOWSTONE
July 15, 1806
J. K. Ralston

The closest the Corps of Discovery came to what is today's Yellowstone National park was the site of present-day Livingston, Montana. Capt. William Clark led a portion of the party through the future site of Livingston on July 15, 1806, the scene pictured here in J. K. Ralston's painting. Clark is shown as the smiling redhead in the foreground, while his slave York has a muzzle-loading rifle slung over his shoulder just to the right of Clark. Sacajawea is holding her baby, Baptiste Charbonneau, between herself and her horse's neck, with Sacajawea's husband/owner Toussaint Charbonneau on a separate horse just behind York and slightly to the left of Sacajawea and Baptiste. Other individuals of Clark's thirteen-member party can be seen strung out into the distance in both directions. The signature west winds of the area are blowing down from the mountains and onto the plains, as shown by the blowing of the horses' manes and Sacajawea's pigtails.

Lewis and Clark did not see any of future Yellowstone Park's remarkable features, but they heard tantalizing references to those wonders from the Native Americans. At various times in their journals the explorers made note of information they received that can be interpreted as references to the Great Falls of the Yellowstone River, as well as other references to the park's renowned geysers.
J. K. RALSTON, ON COMMISSION TO THE FIRST NATIONAL PARK BANK, USED WITH PERMISSION

In this photo on page 54, the fabled mountain men of the Rocky Mountains followed close behind the epic journey of explorers Lewis and Clark, who traveled from St. Louis to the Pacific Ocean and back between May 1804 and September 1806. Imbuing the mountain men as we do with qualities of rugged independence, freedom, courage, toughness, skill in the outdoors, and more, they are a fundamental icon of the region, and elements of the mountain man archetype have segued into all other outdoor figures in the mythology of the American West. With his usual impeccable attention to detail, the incomparable Western artist James Bama has captured a considerable amount of that essence in this 1986 painting titled *Dan, the Mountain Man*. JAMES BAMA

The first Euro-American person we know for certain to have entered what is now Yellowstone Park was John Colter, who, not surprisingly, was a veteran of the Lewis and Clark Expedition. Colter was hired by a St. Louis trader named Manuel Lisa in the summer of 1807 to help establish a seminal fur trapping and trading venture in the Rocky Mountains. In October of that year, Lisa built a trading post at the mouth of the Bighorn River, a major tributary of the Yellowstone River downstream from today's Billings, Montana. The post was called Fort Manuel, and it was from that fort that Lisa dispatched Colter on an epic journey to invite Native Americans to trade at the post, and possibly even to trek as far south as the Spanish settlements in New Mexico.

Probably recruiting Native American guides and horses along the way, Colter likely entered

There are few records of Rocky Mountain fur trappers spending the winter in what is now Yellowstone National Park. This painting, titled *Roche Jaune*, by West Yellowstone artist Gary Carter, one of the most successful works in his renowned career, shows a mounted trapper leading his two packhorses along the rim of the Grand Canyon of the Yellowstone in snowy weather. Probably the mountain man has been caught in the high country by an autumn snowfall and is en route to lower elevations for the winter season.

Roche Jaune means "yellow rock" in French and was the original name bestowed on the Yellowstone River by early-day French Canadian trappers, who were the first Euro-Americans to ever hear anything about the river and the country from which it issued.
GARY CARTER, USED WITH PERMISSION

present-day Yellowstone Park near Cooke City, Montana, traveled down the Lamar River, and then forded the Yellowstone River near Tower Falls on a known indigenous trail. From there he probably traveled southward and exited today's park near its South Entrance. Further evidence indicates that Colter then spent the rest of the winter of 1807–08 on the west side of the Teton Mountain Range in what is today eastern Idaho before trekking back to Fort Manuel via the Bighorn Basin in the spring of 1808.

The strongest evidence we have to indicate that Colter did indeed cross Yellowstone are notations on Capt. William Clark's master maps of 1810 and 1814, which included a tracing of Colter's route past several recognizable landmarks. The tracing on Clark's map is labeled "Colter's Route in 1807," and another telling

Mountain men were known for being independent to the point of defiance. That attitude is reflected here in the mien of the trapper in the foreground of this painting by the legendary Western artist Charles Marion Russell, who is known to have made at least one trip to Yellowstone. The same theme of independence is indicated by the title of the painting—*Free Trapper*. In the mountain man's world, a "free trapper" was a freelancer who trapped on his own and was free to sell his furs to the company offering the best price. That was in contrast to a trapper who, probably not as skilled or as bold, contracted to work for a fur company for the security of a guaranteed wage.

Russell's masterful use of color and light indicate that the season is autumn, as do the tufts of tawny vegetation protruding from the traces of snow on the ground, and the generic scene could be one of many possible settings inside modern-day Yellowstone National Park. Defiant and tough though this trapper and his companions might be, it would have been imperative to descend to lower elevations at this time of year to escape the notoriously ferocious winter of the Rocky Mountain high country. There are many accounts of mountain men traveling through and trapping within the boundaries of what is now Yellowstone National Park, but very few records of any staying inside the park during the winter.
CHARLES MARION RUSSELL

Jim Bridger (top left) was born in 1804, the same year Lewis and Clark embarked on their epic journey of discovery, and did not die until 1881. He spent almost all of his adult life in the West, coming up the Missouri River in 1822 when he was just seventeen years old. The first few decades of his life in the West were spent as a fur trapping mountain man, and he passed through what is now Yellowstone National Park many times during those years in pursuit of peltry.

Joe Meek (top right) came to the Rocky Mountains a little later than Bridger and did not spend as much of his life there, but he was a colorful character who recorded many dramatic adventures during his time as a mountain man. Perhaps his best story in the context of Yellowstone happened when Meek was only nineteen years old. He was traveling with a band of trappers who were attacked and engaged in a pitched battle with the Blackfeet near the Devil's Slide near present-day Gardiner, Montana, just outside the boundary of today's park. Meek became separated from his companions during the melee and wandered south through the mountains for several days before finally setting up his camp one night after dark. The next morning, he climbed a small rise of land nearby, where he saw a sight that moved him to relate to a chronicler many years later: "Behold! The whole country beyond was smoking with the vapor from boiling springs, and burning with gases, issuing from small craters, each of which was emitting a sharp whistling sound." Meek had seen today's Norris Geyser Basin, which he said reminded him of the factories of Pittsburgh (which he apparently had seen earlier in his life). Fortunately for Meek he also came across members of the party from which he had been separated during the battle at Devil's Slide. BEINECKE LIBRARY, YALE UNIVERSITY

Beaver lodge in early winter along the Bechler River in Yellowstone National Park. The beaver brought the mountain men to the Rocky Mountains and the area that became Yellowstone National Park. Hunting aquatic creatures as they did, it was natural for trappers to follow watercourses upstream, and Yellowstone's position as the headwaters of many of the West's major drainage basins naturally led mountain men into the area. The first known Euro-American to travel through the park was John Colter, who ventured here as part of a fur trading endeavor in 1807. From that year onward there are numerous accounts of mountain men traveling through and working in the park. Some of the accounts clearly establish Yellowstone as the location of the trappers' activities, while many other chronicles leave the whereabouts uncertain.

Beavers are fascinating creatures, and the elaborate lodge pictured here is just one example of their industrious handiwork. A closer look reveals a canal the beavers dug leading from their lodge toward the bottom of the photograph. It was probably used during high waters in early summer—the Bechler River is known for flooding almost the entirety of Bechler Meadows when the legendarily deep snows of the region melt in the spring. JEFF HENRY/ROCHE JAUNE PICTURES, INC.

John Colter was a member of the Lewis and Clark Expedition. When the Corps of Discovery was returning to St. Louis in September 1806, Colter asked for his early release from the expedition so he could join two fur trappers who were traveling up the Missouri River to the Rocky Mountains. Colter then stayed in the mountains for four more years, working as a trapper, and in autumn 1807 embarked on an exploratory trek that took him through what is now Yellowstone and Grand Teton National Parks. That Rocky Mountain odyssey took place in the winter of 1807–08, and gives Colter the distinction of being the first Euro-American to see the wonders of the two parks and surrounding areas.

The Colter Stone in this picture was unexpectedly unearthed in 1931 by farmers clearing land near Tetonia, Idaho, on the west side of the Teton Range. One reasonable interpretation of the stone is that Colter carved and incised it while camped and whiling away the worst of the wintry weather. Colter Peak in Yellowstone, Colter Bay on Jackson Lake in Grand Teton National Park, and Colter Pass just outside Yellowstone's Northeast Entrance are three of many place-names that commemorate John Colter's seminal presence in the area. JEFF HENRY/ROCHE JAUNE PICTURES, INC.

label is at Colter's crossing of the Yellowstone River that reads "Hot Springs Brimstone." Historians believe that notation refers to geothermal features Colter saw near his ford across the Yellowstone, a thermal area today known as Calcite Springs, a river crossing that in the years following Colter's time was officially named the Bannock Ford. There is debate about the details of the trek, but everyone would agree that Colter's odyssey is a fundamental element in the lore of Yellowstone.

Very soon after Colter's passage through Yellowstone, other trappers began entering the region in pursuit of fur. Names like Jim Bridger, Kit Carson, Joe Meek, Osborne Russell, and Jim Baker are almost as iconic in the Yellowstone area as John Colter's, and each one of these trappers, along with many others, passed through what is now Yellowstone Park in the early decades of the nineteenth century. Most of them came through the park multiple times, and fortunately for those of us who have an interest in the environment they saw and the lives they led, some of them kept journals that have survived until present times. Joe Meek, Daniel T. Potts, Jim Clyman, Thomas James, Warren Angus Ferris, and others kept journals or at least told their adventures to others who chronicled their stories for them, but the journalist who did the most to elucidate Yellowstone in the early 1800s was Osborne Russell. A good writer who faithfully kept up his diary, he spent much of his nine years in the Rocky Mountains in or near what is now Yellowstone Park. He trapped and camped in the park on three extended expeditions, and among other adventures was attacked and wounded by the Blackfeet at Pelican Creek in 1839. His

John Clymer was an award-winning artist known for the meticulous research he did before even beginning one of his paintings. In this painting, titled *John Colter Visits the Crows*, he depicts John Colter during his epic winter journey through the Yellowstone and Grand Teton country. One interpretation of Colter's trek has him passing south through the site of today's Cody, Wyoming, and from there up the South Fork of the Shoshone River. An interpretation of a further detail has the intrepid explorer meeting the Crows somewhere in the area of the South Fork, and that is the scene Clymer painted in this work. Colter is holding his rifle aloft as an indication of peaceful intentions while making the sign for "talk" with his other hand. Crow warriors are racing out of their camp to confront the interloper, whoever he may be, and their dogs were reacting with hostility, as they were known to do whenever members of a different race appeared. JOHN CLYMER, JOHN CLYMER MUSEUM AND GALLERY, USED WITH PERMISSION

A lone bison walks past erupting Sawmill Geyser at sunset. Warren Angus Ferris was a clerk for the American Fur Company in 1833 when he attended a great rendezvous of trappers held that summer on the Green River in what is now western Wyoming. There he met some mountain men who apparently had traveled through the geyser basins of present-day Yellowstone National Park, and their stories of hot springs and geysers so intrigued him that the following summer Ferris arranged for two American Indians to serve as his guides to the geyser lands. With limited time away from his clerking duties, he and his guides rode hard from their camp west of today's park, and by nightfall on May 19, 1834, arrived in the Upper Geyser Basin. When Ferris awoke the next morning, he saw fields of jetting geysers and hissing hot springs, and was so taken by the scene he wrote in his journal: "The half was not told me." It is impossible to determine exactly where Ferris was when he awoke amid those geothermal wonders, but most historians agree it was in the Upper Geyser Basin and the main geyser he observed was a fountain type that erupts in a series of bursts rather than as a solid column of hot water. It could, then, have been Sawmill Geyser.

Ferris is often credited as being Yellowstone's first tourist, since he came to the area specifically to see the sights rather than for economic reasons. He is further credited with being the first to use the word "geyser" with reference to the eruptive jets of hot water he saw. The Ferris Fork of the Bechler River in the southwestern corner of Yellowstone National Park is named in his honor. JEFF HENRY/ROCHE JAUNE PICTURES, INC.

The Gardner River in Gardner's Hole. Notorious mountain man Johnson Gardner probably came to the Rocky Mountains for the first time in 1822 or 1823. At some later time, he visited this mountain valley in the northern stretches of today's Yellowstone National Park, a valley that now bears his name. The river flowing through the valley is also named for him, as is the town at Yellowstone's North Entrance (although the town spells its name "Gardiner"). Gardner's Hole and the Gallatin Mountains in the background are some of the best places in Yellowstone to look for grizzly bears.

The word "notorious" is used to describe Johnson Gardner because even in the context of the mountain men, many of whom were known for their violent dispositions, Gardner was particularly brutal. In one recorded episode he first scalped and then burned alive two American Indians he had taken captive. JEFF HENRY/ROCHE JAUNE PICTURES, INC.

Potts Hot Springs Basin on the West Thumb of Yellowstone Lake. This thermal area just north around the lakeshore from the better-known West Thumb Geyser Basin was named for Daniel T. Potts, a mountain man originally from Pennsylvania who visited the area in the summer of 1826. Potts wrote three letters to his brother describing Yellowstone Lake and the geothermal features he observed around the lake. His brother sent the missives to the *Philadelphia Gazette* and *Daily Advertiser*, which published an edited account of their contents in its September 27, 1827, edition. The letters were largely forgotten for the next 120 years, until two of Potts's descendants approached the National Park Service in 1947, ultimately selling the letters to the agency. That fortunate event did much to inform historians about the fur trading era in the Rocky Mountains and Yellowstone area.

Potts's descriptions in many ways are similar to those of later travelers to the Yellowstone area. He describes the astonishing clarity of the water in Yellowstone Lake and the lake's location on "the top of a mountain." In common with other reports, he exaggerates the size of the lake, but his descriptions of geothermal activity are accurate and are among the earliest known written records that unmistakably describe the hot springs and geysers within the boundaries of present-day Yellowstone National Park. JEFF HENRY/ROCHE JAUNE PICTURES, INC.

Mammoth Hot Springs is visible for long distances in several directions, so it is not surprising that it was a landmark often mentioned by early-day mountain men. The dramatic formation often appears on early maps, which used information obtained from the intrepid trappers, often with a notation like "Sulphur Mountain" or "Boiling Spring White Sulphur Banks." Its high profile as a landmark for the trappers is understandable, as it is situated only a short distance above the Yellowstone River valley, a frequently used corridor, and very close to the Gardner River, a stream named for well-known mountain man Johnson Gardner and one of the oldest place-names in Yellowstone Park. The great mountain man Jim Bridger, for example, related information about what he called "Sulphur Mountain" on "Gardner's Cr." to Father Pierre-Jean De Smet, a Belgian missionary who drew a map of the West in 1851. Bridger also mentioned the Mammoth formations to Capt. John W. Gunnison, who was a military surveyor who wrote a book in 1852 in which he noted that Bridger described "great Springs, so hot that meat is readily cooked in them, and as they descend on the successive terraces, afford at length delightful baths." JEFF HENRY/ROCHE JAUNE PICTURES, INC.

The Thorofare is the name given to the valley of the upper Yellowstone River above Yellowstone Lake by the mountain men of the early nineteenth century—a name still in use today. And there is magic in that name; a trip to the Thorofare is the ultimate adventure for most park employees and Yellowstone aficionados everywhere. The splendid view of the Thorofare from the top of the Trident (as seen here) is the pinnacle of a Thorofare trip; the vantage is well over 10,000 feet in elevation. The Trident received its name from its three-pronged shape reminiscent of the fearsome pitchfork-like weapon of ancient times. The shaft of the Trident is mostly outside Yellowstone National Park, while most of the three prongs of the feature lie within the park. The Trident is also noteworthy for having precipitously steep sides, almost vertical in places, suggestive of ancient battlements, while the top is relatively flat and primarily treeless tundra. It is a favored habitat of grizzly bears in mid- to late summer. JEFF HENRY/ROCHE JAUNE PICTURES, INC.

Rainbow below the Lower Falls of the Yellowstone. For many years in the nineteenth century, this great falls on the Yellowstone River was called exactly that—the Great Falls of the Yellowstone. Rocky Mountain trappers naturally came this way, following the course of the rivers, and one of them carved his initials into a tree near the falls in 1819. The carving was discovered by Superintendent Philetus W. Norris while on an exploratory excursion through the park in July 1881. Norris recorded that near the falls on "the west side of a smooth pine tree . . . were found, legibly carved through the bark . . . the following: 'J.O.R. August 29, 1819.'" The tree bearing the carving was cut down at some point and the incised section was removed to take to the park's archives, but unfortunately the piece was lost along the way.

Even before J.O.R. carved his initials and date in the pine tree, there was at least one tantalizing reference to the falls. On August 3, 1806, Capt. Meriwether Lewis wrote: "[T]he Indians inform us . . . [that] there is a considerable fall on this river within the mountains . . ." Someone, possibly an editor of Lewis and Clark's journals, later inserted red brackets around the passage, perhaps implying that it was in error. But then as now, the two falls thundered over their brinks, as they have done since the ice of the last ice age melted away. JEFF HENRY/ROCHE JAUNE PICTURES, INC.

Beautiful Indian Pond, located a short distance north of the vastly larger Yellowstone Lake, fills a concavity in the earth left by a steam explosion that possibly occurred when the immense weight of glacial ice melted away from a pocket of geothermal steam pressure that the ice had contained. The pond is surrounded by expanses of lush green meadows, as seen here, and so was a heavily used camping area for Native Americans. Indian Pond received its name because of the obvious signs of their use of the area, which were still visible in 1880 when the observer who gave the little lake its name wrote that there were many brush shelters, wickiups, corrals, and abandoned lodge-poles nearby.

The attractiveness of Indian Pond as a campsite was probably a factor contributing to a pitched battle that occurred there between trappers and Blackfeet in August 1839. A group of forty mountain men, including Baptiste Ducharme, Lou Anderson, Jim and John Baker, Joe Power, and L'Humphrie, traveled north from the Thorofare around the east side of Yellowstone Lake en route to the lake's outlet at today's Fishing Bridge. In the meadows around Indian Pond they encountered a group of Piegans, a subgroup of Blackfeet as resolute as the trappers. According to William T. Hamilton, who recorded the incident in his book *My Sixty Years on the Plains,* a two-day fight ensued.
JEFF HENRY/ROCHE JAUNE PICTURES, INC.

West Yellowstone, Montana, artist Mike Bryers painted this scene, titled *Osborne Russell at Grand Prismatic Spring*, of mountain man Russell and his companions when they came across the feature on July 15, 1839. Osborne Russell was a mountain man in the Yellowstone region from 1834 until 1843 and faithfully kept a journal that is one of the best sources available for telling us about the day-to-day life of a Rocky Mountain trapper during the early years of the nineteenth century. Russell was a good writer and left a spot-on description of the colors that hover in the steam above Grand Prismatic that could have been written by an observer today. He also noted that the water of the great spring was "of deep indigo blue" and "boiling like an immense cauldron." Russell thought Grand Prismatic so intriguing that he presciently wrote: "What a field of speculation this presented for the chemist and geologist." Russell was correct—more than 150 years later National Park Service geologist Rick Hutchinson and his assistants (including this author) would use a specially designed boat to navigate the waters of Grand Prismatic Spring to take temperatures, water samples, and so on. MIKE BRYERS, USED WITH PERMISSION

descriptions of some of the park's primary features are so accurate and well written they are often quoted by today's park tour guides.

～

As much as we are in debt to the chroniclers of the fur trade, many instances in the existing journals tantalizingly hint at major events for which there is no other reference anywhere else in the literature of the fur trade. One example is an 1839 battle between a brigade of forty trappers and a large force of Blackfeet in the meadows around Indian Pond on the north shore of Yellowstone Lake. Five trappers were killed and many others were wounded, while the Blackfeet suffered "the loss of many of their bravest warriors" in the fight that was drawn out over two days. A short mention in a book by William T. Hamilton titled *My Sixty Years on the Plains* is all we know about the pitched battle, even though several recognizable names from the history of the fur trade are listed as participants, and a battle with so many casualties on both sides must have been very big news at the time. Even more frustrating is the realization that if an event as major as the 1839 battle at Indian Pond almost escaped notice, then undoubtedly there were other incidents of comparable or perhaps even greater importance that fur trade chroniclers left out of their records altogether.

Explorers like Lewis and Clark, along with mountain men like Osborne Russell and William T. Hamilton, were the first Euro-Americans to see the wonders of the Yellowstone area, although it goes without saying that their "discoveries" had been known to indigenous peoples for millennia. That said, the early Euro-American travelers did discover Yellowstone within the realm of their own culture, one that very shortly would become dominant not just in the Yellowstone area but across all North America. In the long view of the history of Yellowstone National Park, their most important contribution was the way they passed on what they had seen to mapmakers and explorers who came later, thus becoming an integral link in the evolution of Yellowstone toward its establishment as the world's first national park in 1872.

Of course, an alternative point of view is that the early explorers and the mountain men were just the leading edge of a tidal wave of change and development that overwhelmed the American West with amazing rapidity. White travelers to the Yellowstone area belonged not only to the culture that created Yellowstone and other national parks, but also the culture that created the *need* for parks in the first place by largely eradicating Nature everywhere outside the boundaries of the preserved plots. Nonetheless, it is academically fascinating to trace the evolution of Euro-American knowledge of the Yellowstone area, as well as the greater region around it, by chronologically perusing the progression of maps that appear in the following pages of this book.

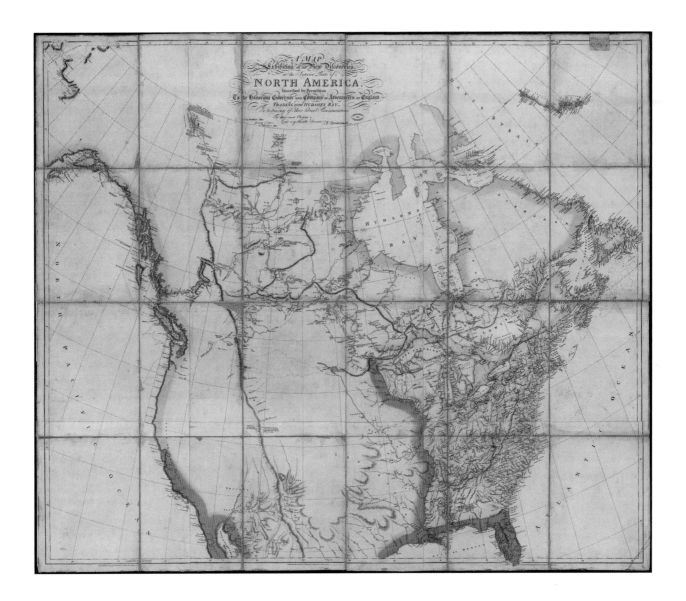

The mountain men of the Rocky Mountain fur trade explored almost every bit of the American West in their pursuit of furs, and the geographic knowledge they gained and then related to others was their biggest contribution to the evolution of the American West that led to the creation of Yellowstone National Park in 1872. This map, produced by English cartographer Aaron Arrowsmith in 1802, and the maps that followed through the nineteenth century and into the early years of the twentieth trace the expansion of knowledge of the American West in general and the Yellowstone area in particular.

Arrowsmith was an Englishman and one of the leading cartographers of his day, and his revised 1802 map of North America was the best that could be had at the time. President Thomas Jefferson relied on the Arrowsmith map while making the Louisiana Purchase, and Lewis and Clark carried a copy on their journey of discovery from 1804 to 1806. A glance at the map shows that it couldn't have been much use to Lewis and Clark, as the entire interior of the American West is essentially blank—it's only value would have been to locate their starting point at St. Louis on the Mississippi River and their ending point at the mouth of the Columbia River on the Pacific Coast. Almost everything in between was simply open space. LIBRARY OF CONGRESS

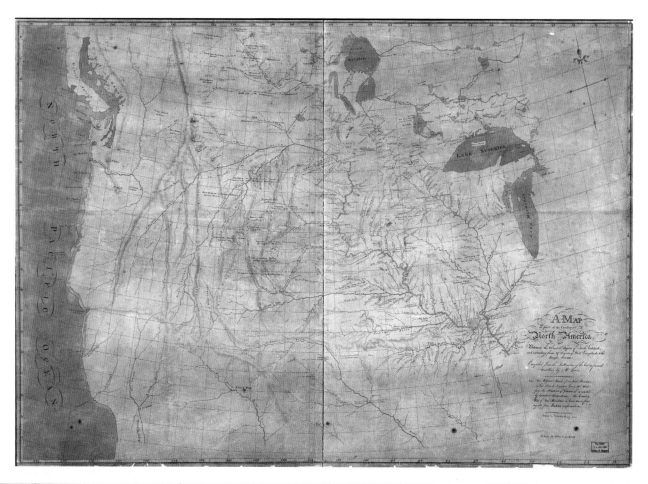

William Clark drew this map through the course of the winter of 1804–05, during the time that Lewis and Clark lived with the Mandans and other tribes at the mouth of the Knife River in what is now western North Dakota. The map incorporated what Lewis and Clark had learned on their trip up the Missouri River to the Mandan villages through the summer of 1804, but west of the Mandans almost all the information came from indigenous sources, so the document is a remarkable reflection on how well they knew the geography of the continent—including areas far removed from their homelands.

Lewis and Clark were meticulous in gathering intelligence for this map, interviewing sources separately and only using information that matched from more than one source. The map, which was sent back to President Jefferson along with other dispatches in the spring of 1805, shows that the Yellowstone River and most of its major tributaries are accurately located. But following upstream along the Yellowstone River from its junction with the Missouri, the viewer can see that as yet there are no hints of the wonders to be seen in the area of today's Yellowstone Park. That said, there is evidence elsewhere that the Native Americans in North Dakota were aware of at least some of those wonders. LIBRARY OF CONGRESS

This map was a prodigious achievement and reflects what Lewis and Clark had learned from their cross-continent journey of 1804–06 as well as information from other travelers through the Rocky Mountain West. Chief among those was John Colter, who was a veteran of the Lewis and Clark Expedition and made his fabled trek through Yellowstone during the winter of 1807–08. Clark's notation of "Colter's Route in 1807" is clearly shown, and landmarks along the route make it clear that Colter did indeed pass through what is now Yellowstone and Grand Teton National Parks. One of the more telling notations on the map is the "Hot Spring Brimstone" near the ford where Colter crossed the Yellowstone. The overwhelming probability is that Colter crossed the well-known ford (later known as Bannock Ford) near Tower Creek, so the "Hot Spring Brimstone" site was almost certainly nearby Calcite Springs. Yellowstone Lake also appears on this 1814 map, bearing the name Lake Eustis, and Jackson Lake on the Snake River is noted as Lake Biddle. Yet another diagnostic notation is the placement of hot springs near the forks of the Shoshone River (labeled "Stinking Water R."), near today's Cody, Wyoming. That is the area known to the trappers and others in the early and middle decades of the nineteenth century as Colter's Hell—that name did *not* refer to the much larger thermal basins in the area of present-day Yellowstone Park. LIBRARY OF CONGRESS

John H. Robinson was a physician who accompanied Zebulon Pike on his 1806 expedition through present-day Kansas and Colorado. Apparently, Robinson also had talent as a cartographer, because he produced this map of the West for publication in 1819. His information came from the Pike Expedition, Lewis and Clark, and others. Noteworthy in the context of Yellowstone is how Robinson used yellow highlight to trace the routes of travelers through the Northern Rockies; most relevant is the route shown just to the west of the present park taken by Peter Weiser. Like Colter, Weiser was a veteran of the Lewis and Clark Expedition engaged in the fur trade after completion of the expedition. Evidence strongly suggests that he traveled up the Madison River from the Three Forks of the Missouri, crossed the Continental Divide via Raynolds Pass, and then entered the Snake River valley. A "Weiser's River" appears on the Robinson map along the upper reaches of the Snake, and at the very least Weiser passed within a few miles of the boundary of today's Yellowstone National Park on his way to the upper Snake River. Given the fact that he was out scouting for trapping territory, it's not unreasonable to think that he may have traveled farther up the Madison toward its sources. If so, he may very well have entered what is today the park. LIBRARY OF CONGRESS

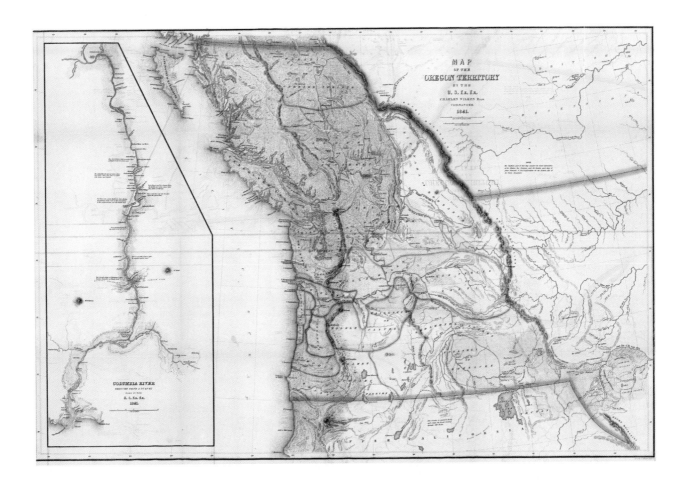

Charles Wilkes was a US naval officer who traveled and explored widely around the entire world. He produced this map, which includes some new details in the immediate Yellowstone area, in 1841. There is a notation for a "Steam Spring" just downstream on the Yellowstone River from the outlet of Sublette's Lake (today's Yellowstone Lake). That could possibly be the Mud Volcano area, or any of several other thermal basins along that stretch of the river, but it does reflect that more information had come forth about Yellowstone, probably via fur trappers. There is also a "Hot Sulphur Springs" on the Wilkes map some distance downriver from Sublette's Lake, which is likely Mammoth Hot Springs. Another development of regional knowledge is that Jackson Lake, south of Yellowstone, had received its present name on this map, and importantly is shown to drain to the south and west via the Snake River. Earlier maps had shown the lake, then called Lake Biddle, as forming the head of the Wind River and consequently draining to the south and then east. LIBRARY OF CONGRESS

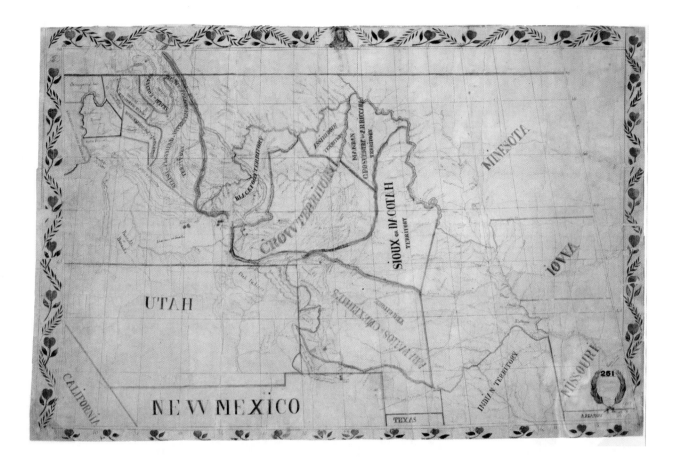

This is one of the most important maps in the evolution of geographical knowledge of Yellowstone. In 1851 a council of Native American tribes and government bureaucrats was held on Horse Creek in the southeastern part of what later became Wyoming. Jim Bridger, the greatest mountain man of them all, was there, as was Father Pierre-Jean De Smet, a Catholic priest from Belgium who spent much of his life in North America, and much of that on the western frontier. The 1851 map was drawn by De Smet at the Horse Creek Council, and it is clear that Bridger was the source of much of what was included on the map.

The map has many notations about "volcanic" activity, including one describing a volcanic region one hundred miles wide.

It also locates Bridger Lake and is one of the first maps to label Yellowstone Lake as such, although De Smet wrote "Yellowstone or Sublette's Lake," referring to what the lake had been called by mountain men for about thirty years by 1851. And there is yet another reference to today's Mammoth Hot Springs, still called by De Smet the "Sulphur Springs" on the "Gardener River." This is definitely a direct link to Bridger—the Gardner River, as it is spelled today, was named for Johnson Gardner, a mountain man whose career in the Rockies dated back to the early 1820s, and therefore a man Bridger probably knew well. LIBRARY OF CONGRESS

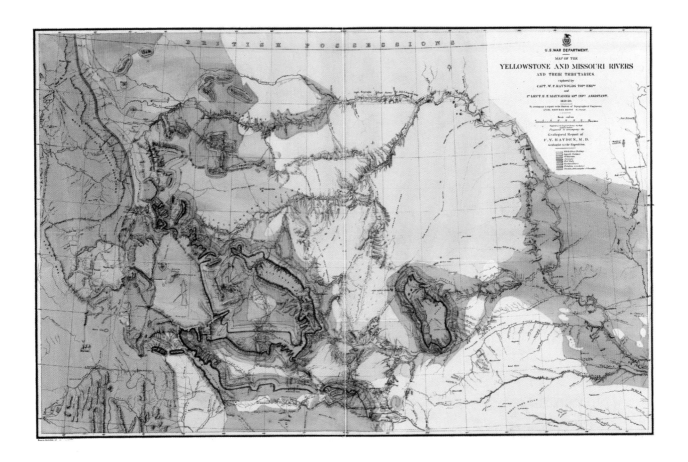

Captain William F. Raynolds was a US Army officer dispatched in 1859 to explore and map the regions that later became the states of Montana and Wyoming. After spending the winter of 1859–60 along the Platte River in central Wyoming, Raynolds set out to ascend the Wind River to the high Rockies, hoping to cross over the mountains from the upper Wind River to the upper Yellowstone River. Jim Bridger, who seemed to be ubiquitous in the early days of the West, was hired by Raynolds in one of the smartest moves he made on his whole trip. Along the way Bridger told Raynolds it would not be possible to travel through the high country between the upper Wind and the upper Yellowstone so early in the year because of lingering snowpack. That turned out to be the case, so Raynolds and his party skirted the southern and western boundaries of the present park en route to the Three Forks of the Missouri. Raynolds did leave this map, which of course shows a great deal of influence from Bridger. LIBRARY OF CONGRESS

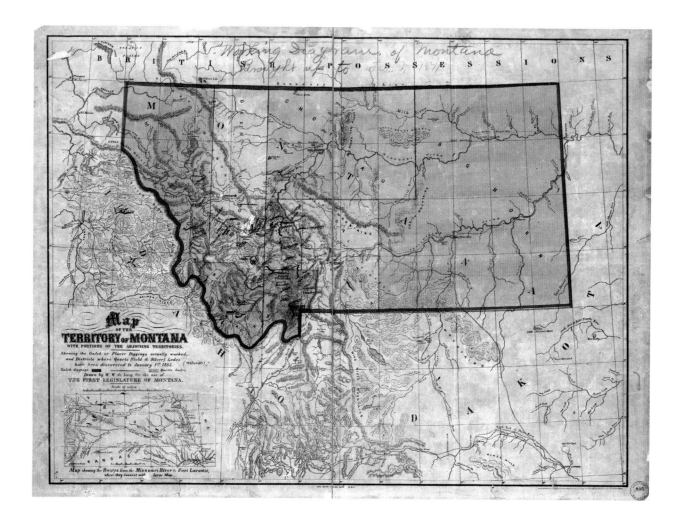

Walter Washington DeLacy led a party of gold seekers into what is now Yellowstone National Park in 1865. The party entered the area from the south and passed through the Firehole River valley on their way to the Madison River, which they followed downriver to mining settlements in the Montana Territory. The information on DeLacy's map reflects this route. A large lake they named DeLacy Lake (today's Shoshone Lake) is shown in oblong form north of Jackson's Lake. There are two notations for hot springs along the waterways in the southern part of the park, which indicates that the party saw the thermal features along the upper Snake River, especially those of the Shoshone Geyser Basin at the west end of Shoshone Lake. Noteworthy also is the notation "Hot Spring Valley" north of Shoshone Lake, which refers to the great geyser basins along the Firehole River valley.

The DeLacy party did not see the eastern stretches of Yellowstone Park, so there is only a rough depiction of Yellowstone Lake and a hashmark across the Yellowstone River labeled "Falls."

DeLacy's 1865 map was widely circulated in Montana Territory and led to further explorations and greater knowledge of the Yellowstone area, which within just a few years led to the establishment of Yellowstone as a national park. LIBRARY OF CONGRESS

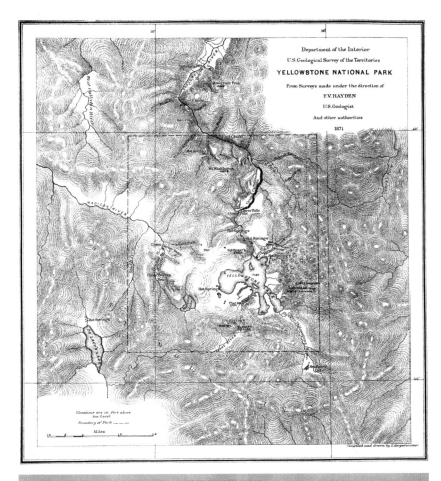

This map is the result of the 1871 Hayden Survey through the Yellowstone area. It is better than any earlier map at depicting many recognizable features in the park, and many of the names inscribed on the map are the names still in use today. The Hayden Survey and the information it collected led directly and quickly (only about seven months after the survey was conducted) to the establishment of Yellowstone National Park. LIBRARY OF CONGRESS

Produced by the US Geological Survey, this 1915 map reflects the Yellowstone Park that we know today. The geographic information is correct, and each feature is in the correct place relative to other features. The road network is mostly the same as today, and a closer look reveals that even many of the developed properties that we know today were already in existence: The Lake Yellowstone Hotel and the Old Faithful Inn, for example, had already been constructed and open for business for quite a few years. It had been only a little more than a century since John Colter had made his trek through Yellowstone in 1807, before which time it is almost certain that no other Euro-American had ever seen the area. LIBRARY OF CONGRESS

CHAPTER 4
PROSPECTING ERA

One legacy of gold mining in the Yellowstone region is the abandoned mining equipment, devastated landscapes, and polluted water that miners left behind when their claims played out. Fortunately, there is not much in the way of impacted ecosystems and toxic leavings within the boundaries of Yellowstone Park itself, but as this photograph shows, such problems exist just a short distance away. This image was taken in 1994 at the head of Fisher Creek just east of Cooke

City, Montana, outside the park. It is worth noting, however, that the polluted waters of Fisher Creek feed into Soda Butte Creek, which in turn flows into Yellowstone Park and ultimately joins the Lamar River. Fortunately, efforts in recent years have restored many such mining-impacted areas and also reduced the amount of polluted runoff. JEFF HENRY/ROCHE JAUNE PICTURES, INC.

PROSPECTORS BEGAN ENTERING THE YELLOWSTONE REGION in the early 1860s. They came primarily from Montana Territory, where gold had been discovered in 1862. In common with all early-day gold rushes, Montana's easily recovered surface deposits quickly played out, so prospectors had to move on to look for new finds. Because of the Montana goldfields' relative proximity to Yellowstone, it was natural that they soon moved into the area that just a few years later would be designated the world's first national park. There they became some of the first Euro-Americans after the earlier trappers to see the area's natural wonders. Indeed, it should be pointed out that prospectors relied on geographic information they inherited directly or indirectly from the fur trappers, many of whom were still alive when the prospecting era

Double rainbow over the mouth of Black Canyon of the Yellowstone River. Most prospecting parties of the 1860s and 1870s entered the park area via the Yellowstone River valley. The valley not only offered the most geographically feasible travel corridor, but waterways were where nineteenth-century prospectors searched for placer deposits of gold. The Black Canyon of the Yellowstone, in the parlance of the prospectors, was the Third Canyon of the river. They numbered the canyons of the river as they passed upstream, with the First Canyon being the one just south of Livingston, Montana; the Second Canyon the one we call Yankee Jim Canyon, about thirteen miles north of Yellowstone's North Entrance; the Third Canyon being the Black; and finally the Fourth Canyon the one we call the Grand Canyon of the Yellowstone River. JEFF HENRY/ROCHE JAUNE PICTURES, INC.

commenced. Jim Bridger, for one, was present at various times in Montana gold mining towns like Virginia City, where there is an 1866 record of him providing a very good description of an erupting geyser in the Yellowstone country.

One of the first prospecting expeditions to enter what is now Yellowstone National Park was led by Walter Washington DeLacy, who was a civil engineer by profession. DeLacy started out with a party of forty prospectors, but his 1863 expedition soon splintered into factions that more or less went their separate ways. The portion of the party still under DeLacy's direct leadership traveled up today's Lewis River in the southern part of Yellowstone Park, a course that led them to Lewis Lake and then to Shoshone Lake. From

Knowles Falls on the Yellowstone River in Black Canyon. Knowles Falls was one of the most prominent features in Black Canyon that gold prospectors came across on their travel upstream. Fortunately for the gold seekers, there was a heavily used trail made by Native Americans that passed up the river on its north side (the left side of the river from the viewpoint of this photograph). JEFF HENRY/ROCHE JAUNE PICTURES, INC.

This photograph, shot by renowned pioneer photographer William Henry Jackson, shows a miner panning for gold near Virginia City, Montana. It also shows the devastation that mining often wrought on the landscape, even with the comparatively primitive technology of the 1860s. WILLIAM HENRY JACKSON, NATIONAL ARCHIVES

there they passed through a stretch of heavily forested country to the Firehole River, where they saw the profuse hot springs and geysers of the Upper Geyser Basin (they had already seen similar if less grandiose thermal features in the Shoshone Geyser Basin). From the great geyser basins along the Firehole the party traveled down the Madison River and eventually out of today's park on their way back to the Montana settlements.

Present-day place-names DeLacy Lake and DeLacy Creek commemorate this trip, but more important to the history of Yellowstone National Park was how DeLacy's expedition returned with new information about the country surrounding the upper Madison River and upper Snake River drainages. Undoubtedly the

Artist Todd Fredricksen of Gardiner, Montana, drew this sketch of a nineteenth-century prospector panning for gold in the Firehole River where it flows through the Upper Geyser Basin. Prospectors found gold in many places inside what is today Yellowstone National Park, but very few, if any, of those finds were inside the great Yellowstone caldera. As the Upper Geyser Basin is well inside the caldera, this prospector's efforts probably produced nothing in the way of "color," which is how prospectors described the appearance of gold dust in the bottom of their pans. TODD FREDRICKSEN, USED WITH PERMISSION

Asahel Curtis (1874–1941) was a lifelong photographer who specialized in subjects in Alaska and the Pacific Northwest. He did, however, shoot and market many photos of Yellowstone Park. This photo was made during the Alaska gold rush in 1898, but it can also be viewed as illustrative of a solitary prospector leading his pack animals through the dense coniferous forests of Yellowstone. ASAHEL CURTIS, WIKIPEDIA COMMONS

THE FIRST GOLD-HUNTERS.

This drawing was done in 1860 and shows a scene from the California gold rush, which predated the era of prospecting in the Yellowstone area. But, like the previous photograph by Asahel Curtis, it serves to illustrate a scene that could have and almost certainly did happen in Yellowstone. *HARPER'S NEW MONTHLY (APRIL 1860),* WIKIPEDIA COMMONS

new geographic knowledge spread quickly to other miners around the Montana boomtowns. Moreover, DeLacy had experience as a cartographer, and in 1865 he produced a map of Montana Territory and its surrounding areas, which of course included information gained on his trip up the Snake River and down the Madison from its headwaters. Members of at least one later prospecting trip are recorded as having used DeLacy's map while navigating through the Yellowstone country in 1867—the party of a mysterious but important figure in Yellowstone history named A. Bart Henderson. His party used the map to identify Yellowstone Lake, which they spotted from a high point just south of the present park's southern boundary.

Similar prospecting parties ventured out of the Montana settlements and ranged to the south in 1864. Two parties actually traveled far to the south of Yellowstone before turning back north and passing through the eastern portions of today's park. In yet another tidbit linking the prospector era to the mountain men, both groups followed an old trapper trail over Two Ocean Pass and then down the Yellowstone River before passing around the east side of Yellowstone Lake on a route that ultimately took them out of the park near today's North Entrance at Gardiner, Montana. An early frontiersman with the colorful name Adam "Horn" Miller was a member of one of these groups, and he added an important place-name to Yellowstone as his party traveled along the shores of Yellowstone Lake: After one of his companions shot a pelican at the mouth of a major tributary to the lake, Miller fittingly named the stream Pelican Creek. Also notable was how Horn Miller and his companions found the fresh trails of other prospecting parties when they reached the mouth of the Lamar River—by 1864 it seems that numerous parties were passing through today's Yellowstone on their search for gold.

The very nature of prospecting for placer deposits of gold was similar to the work done by the earlier beaver trappers in that both endeavors were oriented toward water, so the geographical knowledge accumulated by both the trappers and the prospectors was slanted toward watercourses and stream valleys. There was also a motivation in both endeavors to travel ever higher up rivers and streams in an effort to find new, unexploited waters; so given the headwaters character of Yellowstone's high country, it is almost certain that both the trappers and the prospectors reached the park area fairly early in their respective tenures. It was also true that the nature of both pursuits inclined their participants toward secrecy—to

Well-known Hellroaring Creek is one of several streams that head in country outside the northern boundary of Yellowstone, then flow south into the park and feed into the Yellowstone River in the Black Canyon. Nineteenth-century prospectors found gold in virtually all these streams, and, not surprisingly, Hellroaring Creek received its name from a prospecting party that traveled up the Yellowstone in 1867. JEREMY SCHMIDT, NATIONAL PARK SERVICE

avoid leaking information about good places to trap beavers or pan for gold—so there is a paucity of historical records from both eras. Another similarity is that frequent hints appear in the scanty literature that does exist indicating there were other exploratory parties out at the same time as the chronicled expeditions, though no records of these other parties were kept (at least no records that survived until the present).

In the years after 1864, there were so many prospecting parties passing through the Yellowstone country that it is not possible to list all of them here. But because of several magical names its members placed on the landscape of Yellowstone's northern tier, one expedition in 1867, led by a man named Lou Anderson, is worth noting. Anderson, who may have been in the Yellowstone area as early as 1850 in the company

The famous Charles Russell painted this scene of the 1864 discovery of gold at Last Chance Gulch. The name came from the legend that the prospectors who found gold in the gulch that later became downtown Helena, Montana, were taking their last chance before giving up their hopes for riches and returning home. It was the development of goldfields elsewhere in Montana that led to the exploration of the Yellowstone area by many of the same prospectors, and the knowledge they gained led directly to the establishment of Yellowstone National Park just a few years later. CHARLES MARION RUSSELL, GILCREASE MUSEUM, TULSA, OKLAHOMA

Two prospectors pan for gold in Nelson Gulch near Helena, Montana, in the 1860s.
LIBRARY OF CONGRESS

Father Xavier Kuppens was a Jesuit priest from Belgium who spent much of his career in early-day Montana. During the winter of 1864–65 he was living with American Indians, who related to him descriptions of some of the wonders of the Yellowstone area. Kuppens managed to enlist several of the Blackfeet to serve as his guides to the region the following summer—yet another illustration of how well the Native Americans knew the area. The winter following his excursion to Yellowstone, Father Kuppens was living with some Blackfeet near the site of today's Great Falls, Montana, when a severe blizzard hit. Several travelers who were a who's who of pioneering Montanans became stranded at Kuppens's establishment, and the stories he and the Blackfeet and an old trapper who was married to a Blackfeet woman told piqued the interest of the travelers, who were socially positioned to influence further explorations of the Yellowstone area. YELLOWSTONE NATIONAL PARK COLLECTION

John Curl, Adam "Horn" Miller, and Joe Brown were pioneering prospectors in the Yellowstone area, and stories about them are part of the bedrock of the region. That they were tough, resourceful, and independent is not debatable, and cultural respect for these and other prospectors is reflected in the wide range of place-names still in existence that were placed on the landscape by these and similar men. And for Adam "Horn" Miller and Joe Brown, at least, there are many places in the Yellowstone area that were named directly in their honor. YELLOWSTONE NATIONAL PARK COLLECTION

"Yellowstone Jack" Baronett was born in Scotland in 1827 and became a sailor and a world traveler at an early age. He had experience as a gold seeker in California, Australia, and Africa before arriving in the Yellowstone region in 1864. He worked as a prospector in this area for several years, while at the same time developing a well-deserved reputation as a knowledgeable and capable man. Because of that reputation he was recruited to search for Truman Everts, a member of the 1870 Washburn Expedition to Yellowstone, who became separated from his companions and spent thirty-seven starving days in the wilderness before Baronett and George Pritchett found him and saved his life. Shortly after finding Everts, Baronett began working on this bridge over the Yellowstone River just upstream from its junction with the Lamar. First opened for business in 1871, the bridge, which was the first to span the Yellowstone anywhere along its length, was an important development on the trail between Montana settlements and the mineral diggings in the New World Mining District just outside the Northeast Entrance to Yellowstone National Park. YELLOWSTONE NATIONAL PARK COLLECTION

of Kit Carson and Jim Bridger, and who may even have been present at the big battle between trappers and Blackfeet at Indian Pond in 1839, was inspired to prospect the area because of an earlier gold discovery at the downstream end of what trappers and prospectors called the Second Canyon of the Yellowstone River (today's Black Canyon). That discovery had been made at the mouth of Bear Creek, in late summer 1866, by Joe Brown, another famous character in Yellowstone's history.

Traveling up the Yellowstone River on its east or north bank, the Anderson party stopped and investigated the first major stream they encountered above the mouth of Bear Creek. Their naming of that stream was recorded thusly: "We found $9,000 in gold in a crevice at the mouth of the creek, so we named it Crevice Creek." After exhausting the deposits in Crevice Creek, the same party continued up the Yellowstone, each day sending a man named A. H. Hubble ahead to scout the trail and evaluate the next stream crossing. One evening, after returning to camp from his daily reconnoiter, Hubble was asked about

"Uncle" John Yancey was born in Kentucky in 1826 and came to the Yellowstone Park area sometime around 1870. He worked as a prospector and evidently stuck enough pay dirt to establish a hotel in Pleasant Valley near the site of Yellowstone Jack Baronett's bridge over the Yellowstone River. The hotel, which is just out of frame to the left in this photo by pioneering photographer Frank J. Haynes, was well situated on the trail between settlements in western Montana and the Cooke City mining districts just outside the northeastern corner of Yellowstone National Park. Yancey's hotel was an important stopover for travelers on the Cooke City trail, and as travel within the park increased in the latter years of the nineteenth century it became an important way station for tourists as well. Yancey himself is visible in this scene, standing to the left of the marching line of soldiers, while photographer Haynes is thought to be the figure on the light colored horse at the head of the column. YELLOWSTONE NATIONAL PARK COLLECTION

President Bill Clinton came to Yellowstone in 1996 to announce a ban on large-scale mining operations in the Cooke City area, just outside Yellowstone National Park's Northeast Entrance. He is pictured here speaking at a press conference that was used to make the announcement. Yellowstone National Park's then superintendent Mike Finley stands just to the right of the president, wearing the classic Stetson hat of the National Park Service. One of Clinton's most memorable statements during the press conference was that "Yellowstone is more precious than gold." JIM PEACO, YELLOWSTONE NATIONAL PARK COLLECTION

the nature of the next watercourse. His answer was, "It's a real hell roarer," and hence the name Hellroaring Creek came to be. He returned similarly a day or so later and described the next stream crossing as "but a slough," although the water of Slough Creek, far from being placid, turned out to be so powerful that the company lost a packhorse and its load when the animal was swept away in the torrent. Over a short span of time, three landmark streams, all of which begin their courses outside the boundaries of Yellowstone before flowing into the park, received their iconic names.

~

It's hard to overstate the role of gold prospecting and gold rushes in the pioneering history of the American West. Prospectors flocked to goldfields, increasing the Euro-American population in the area of the new diggings not just with their own numbers, but also by attracting many others who came west to support those who sought gold. In the case of Yellowstone, prospecting and mining brought large numbers of people into the area just north of the park. Prospectors branched out from those goldfields in Montana into the area that was later designated the park, collecting and disseminating geographic information about the country to others, and in some cases actually producing maps of the area that was new to most Americans. Additionally, the official exploration parties that were soon to investigate the wonders of Yellowstone used the nearby Montana mining communities as bases for their expeditions. Beyond that, many of the miners later actually served as guides, or in some cases leaders, of the official exploration parties that were soon to come to the park, and which in turn led directly to the creation of Yellowstone as a national park on March 1, 1872.

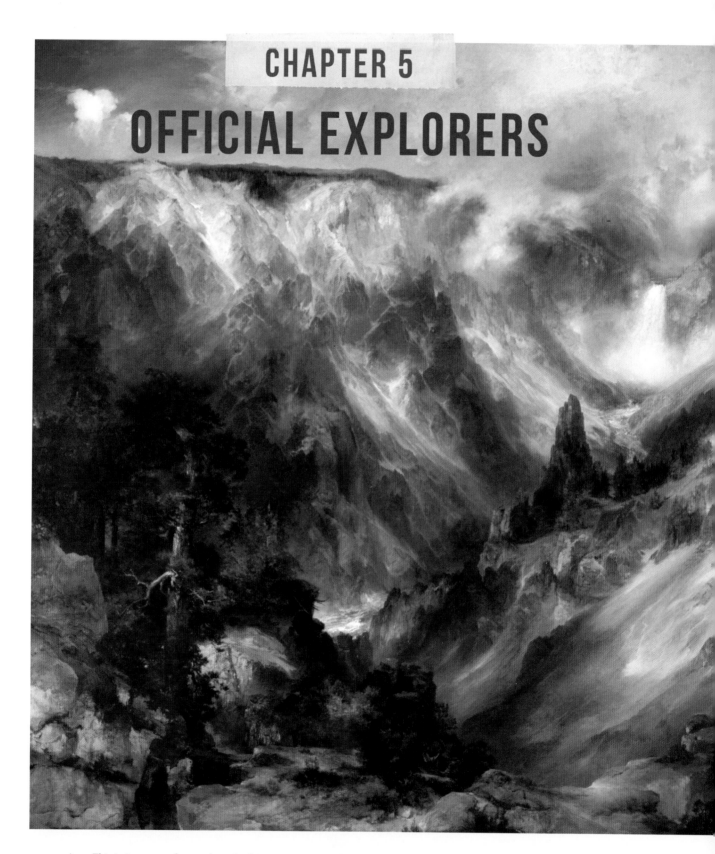

CHAPTER 5
OFFICIAL EXPLORERS

This is just one of many breathtaking paintings produced by Thomas Moran as a result of his tour through Yellowstone with the Hayden Survey in 1871. As a beautiful rendition of the storied Great Falls of the Yellowstone, what we call the Lower Falls today, it was probably one of his most impactful works, leading to public and government support for the creation of Yellowstone National Park. THOMAS MORAN, SMITHSONIAN INSTITUTION

THE FIRST ORGANIZED, OFFICIAL EXPLO-RATION PARTY specifically intended to investigate what is now Yellowstone National Park was the Raynolds Expedition of 1859 and 1860. Raynolds was a career army officer who graduated from West Point in 1843 and almost immediately was assigned to a branch of the military charged with surveying and mapping duties. Experience in that sort of work was probably the reason the US War Department, on April 13, 1859, selected him to "organize an expedition for the exploration of the region of country through which flow the principal tributaries of the Yellowstone river [*sic*], and of the mountains in which they, and the Gallatin and Madison forks of the Missouri, have their sources." The entire region Raynolds was directed to explore was much larger than just those listed streams and mountains—in

Hayden Party on Horses in Upper Geyser Basin depicts the moment when members of the 1871 Hayden Survey of Yellowstone arrived in the Upper Geyser Basin. Interestingly, the painting was done many years after the occurrence, and even more interestingly it was painted by William Henry Jackson, not the better-known artist of the Hayden party, Thomas Moran. Jackson was the photographer on the Hayden trip, but many years later he taught himself to paint and rendered a number of scenes of his earlier days spent exploring Yellowstone. The scene shown in this work has a geyser erupting on the far side of the Firehole River from the mounted explorers and is probably Jackson's remembrance of Grand Geyser. It is known that Grand erupted just as the explorers arrived on the scene in early August 1871. YELLOWSTONE NATIONAL PARK COLLECTION

This is another painting done late in life by former photographer William Henry Jackson. It shows the 1871 Hayden Survey riding along the beach of Yellowstone Lake at Bridge Bay. The scene is near today's Bridge Bay Campground and Marina, and accurately depicts the layout of the Absaroka Mountains on the east side of the lake. Gull Point is also accurately located at the right on the far side of Bridge Bay, but the island in the center of the frame, almost certainly intended to represent Stevenson Island, is placed too far to the viewer's left, or north of its actual location. YELLOWSTONE NATIONAL PARK COLLECTION

his own writings Raynolds later noted that the tract he was assigned to investigate was one-fourth larger than the whole of France, amounting to about 250,000 square miles in all—which makes you wonder whether the issuers of the War Department directive to Raynolds had some inkling of the unusual characteristics of those particular areas around the heads of the Yellowstone and Missouri Rivers. Given that there were already in existence a number of accounts and maps from fur traders, missionaries, and others that hinted at features like hot springs, geysers, mountains of sulfur, and more, it seems reasonable that they did.

In what might have been his most astute move during the entire expedition, Captain Raynolds hired Jim Bridger as his guide. The history of the American West is an intertwined network of connections between individuals and eras, and an amazing number of those threads wind through the great Jim Bridger, who was in the West from

Early-day travelers to Yellowstone almost always supplemented their food stocks with wild game and fish (which was legal at the time), an approach that made sense because of the area's remoteness. These hunters were probably with the Hayden Survey of 1872, and the photo shows five bull elk they killed near Canyon. The location is interesting because that same area is preferred summer habitat for bull elk today. WILLIAM HENRY JACKSON, YELLOWSTONE NATIONAL PARK COLLECTION

1822 until the late 1860s. He lived in the West so long that he bridged the time between some of the earliest fur trading expeditions and the era of official exploration of what became Yellowstone National Park.

The geologist assigned to the 1859–60 Raynolds Expedition was none other than Ferdinand V. Hayden, who, a little more than a decade after the Raynolds trip, led his own official surveys to Yellowstone. Hayden in turn publicized his finds, which were instrumental in having Yellowstone designated a national park. In the journals of the Raynolds Expedition, it is clear that Hayden spent much time with Bridger, often just one on one while they rode together across the western landscapes. Hayden must have heard a lot from Bridger that piqued his interest about the country around the heads of the Madison and Yellowstone Rivers.

After hiring Bridger, the Raynolds Expedition spent the summer of 1859 exploring the Lower

Yellowstone River and its southern tributaries before retiring to winter camp on the Platte River in what is now central Wyoming. In the spring of 1860 Raynolds divided his command, sending a small detachment under Lt. Henry E. Maynadier down the Bighorn River while he led a larger contingent up the Wind River toward the spine of the Rocky Mountains. The intended rendezvous of the two parties was the Three Forks of the Missouri, where they planned to meet by June 30 to make observations of a solar eclipse that was predicted to occur in July. The timing of this rendezvous was to have ironic implications for Raynolds's hopes of investigating reports from Bridger and others regarding the wonders of the Upper Yellowstone and Upper Madison Rivers.

Captain Raynolds's plan was to cross from the head of the Wind River to the ultimate head of the Yellowstone River south of Yellowstone Lake. From the beginning Bridger told him that because

Along with the paintings produced by Thomas Moran, William Henry Jackson's large-format photographs played a pivotal role in the establishment of Yellowstone as a park in 1872. Here a mounted Jackson is pictured on the very top of Mount Washburn with the pack mule bearing his photographic supplies. This shot from the 1871 Hayden Survey illustrates the great efforts Jackson had to make to produce his photographs—he had packed up all his cumbersome photo equipment onto a mule and then ridden to the summit of 10,243-foot Mount Washburn while leading the mule. WILLIAM HENRY JACKSON, YELLOWSTONE NATIONAL PARK COLLECTION

Photographer William Henry Jackson and artist Thomas Moran naturally spent a lot of time together during their sojourn in Yellowstone with the Hayden Survey of 1871. Here Jackson posed Moran on Jupiter Terrace of Mammoth Hot Springs to lend a human dimension and an element of scale to his composition. The peak in the distance is Sheep Mountain, which is outside the boundaries of today's Yellowstone and due north of the park's North Entrance. WILLIAM HENRY JACKSON, YELLOWSTONE NATIONAL PARK COLLECTION

of deep snows and the appallingly rugged terrain between the sources of the two rivers, such a route would not be possible so early in the season. Interestingly, Raynolds's journal entries about Bridger waver back and forth between denigrating Bridger because of his rough and uneducated nature, and then raving about the old mountain man's extensive and detailed knowledge of the country through which the expedition was passing. In this case Raynolds did not accept Bridger's prediction about the impassable nature of the high country between the two rivers, noting that it had to be quicker to make the direct approach to the headwaters of the Yellowstone from the Upper Wind River than it would to take the wide arc to the west that Bridger recommended, a route that clearly was much longer but avoided the higher, snowier country on the direct route. Bridger, of course, was correct, and the expedition spent a lot of effort and time thrashing around in the deep snows of the high Absaroka Retain Range before turning south and passing over Union Pass and into the drainage of the Pacific Ocean.

Still intent on reaching the valley of the Upper Yellowstone, Raynolds spent more time and effort trying to access the valley from its west side. Once again stymied by deep snow and difficult terrain, and also running out of time before his scheduled rendezvous to observe the solar eclipse at the Three Forks of the Missouri, Raynolds at last had to give up. He and his party descended the Gros Ventre River into Jackson's Hole, recording in his journal that his "expedition passed entirely around [the thermal region], but could not penetrate it," and so he and his men were "compelled to content ourselves with listening to marvelous tales [mostly from Jim Bridger] of burning plains, immense lakes, and boiling springs, without being able to verify these wonders."

The Raynolds Expedition then left Jackson's Hole over Teton Pass and journeyed north to Henry's Lake. From there the expedition crossed the Continental Divide again over the gentle gap in the mountains that ever since has been known as Raynolds Pass, and then made its way down the Madison River to the Three Forks. Ironically, the other arm of the Raynolds Expedition, the one commanded by Lieutenant Maynadier, was late arriving at the rendezvous point, so the planned observations of the solar eclipse, which cut short Raynolds's time in the Yellowstone country, were not made. Had Raynolds known, he could have spent more time waiting for the snow to melt in the Yellowstone high country and feasibly could have made a tour of the area's geyser basins, as he had so desired to do.

One more anecdote from the Raynolds Expedition is worth mentioning. While passing by Henry's Lake at the head of the Henry's Fork of the Snake River, Ferdinand Hayden and three others made a side trip to Targhee Pass, a pass that leads from the Henry's Fork in the basin of the Pacific Ocean to the Madison River on the Atlantic side of the divide. Two of Hayden's companions on that junket are not identified, but one of them could have been Jim Bridger himself. At the very least it must have been Bridger who directed Hayden and the others to the five-mile route they had to take from Henry's Lake to Targhee Pass, and Bridger is recorded in Raynolds's journal as giving a good description of the country that could be seen to the east from the top of the pass, including much of the western part of today's Yellowstone National Park. Especially if Bridger was one of the four, what an image that must have been: Ferdinand Hayden, Jim Bridger, and the others, one of whom may have been a soldier from Raynolds's military detachment, sitting on their horses on top of that beautiful mountain pass, looking wistfully toward the great geyser basins and other wonders of the Yellowstone Plateau. If the image is accurate, Bridger was probably sitting on his

Another painting by Thomas Moran, this one showing Crested Pool in the foreground and an erupting Castle Geyser with members of the 1871 Hayden Expedition watching in close proximity. Yellowstone can be seen as both dynamic and timeless, and in this scene seems more the latter—both Crested Pool and Castle Geyser look the same today as they did in Moran's dramatic painting. THOMAS MORAN, WIKIPEDIA COMMONS

horse thinking back to the days when he was a young man in the heyday of the Rocky Mountain fur trade, while Hayden the geologist must have been yearning to explore the improbable features he'd heard about from Bridger and others.

~

Chronologically, the next expedition to Yellowstone that is often described as an official endeavor was actually only somewhat so. By 1869 David Folsom, Charles Cook, and William Peterson had spent time in the Montana goldfields around Helena and in Confederate Gulch. They had been moderately successful in the mining business, but were not really at the top of evolving Montana society. In this regard they fit the general trend of Yellowstone explorers: As time went on and the Yellowstone country became safer and better known, and as it became more and more apparent that some sort of special importance was attached to the area, the social elite began inserting themselves more into affairs involving Yellowstone. In 1869 that trend was just beginning its evolution, so the Folsom-Cook-Peterson Expedition, mounted by these three men from the mid-levels of Montana society, was the only even quasi-official party to take the field that year.

Albert Bierstadt was a famous landscape artist of the mid- to late nineteenth century. His reputation was well established by the time Yellowstone National Park was created in 1872, and while he did not accompany any of the official exploration parties through the area, many proponents of the park idea were eager to have Bierstadt come and paint some of his epic works as a way to boost support for the creation. Those park proponents were successful in arranging for Bierstadt to visit, as evidenced by his interpretation of the Lower Falls of the Yellowstone River reproduced here. ALBERT BIERSTADT, WIKIPEDIA COMMONS

Albert Bierstadt was especially enthralled by Yellowstone's geysers, and he painted this beauti-ful scene of Old Faithful Geyser with the foreground element of the Firehole River composition-ally leading to the erupting geyser, probably in the 1870s. So taken was he by the Yellowstone geysers, Bierstadt wrote, "I have never been so impressed with the infinite divinity of the types of nature as I was by the . . . geysers." ALBERT BIERSTADT, WIKIART

The expedition left the Montana settlements in mid-September, a little late in the year to embark on such a journey into the Yellowstone high country. One reason for the late start was that other, more socially elite members of Montana society had indeed contemplated going on the trip but then began dropping out as the summer progressed. Troubles with the Sioux and the Cheyenne along the Bozeman Trail, one of the main thoroughfares used by Euro-American travelers to and from the Montana goldfields, spooked the more elite members of society in the newly created territory. And when a hoped-for military escort failed to materialize because the soldiers were assigned to address real or imagined dangers from Native Americans elsewhere, everyone who had been interested in the Yellowstone trip dropped out—except for Folsom, Cook, and Peterson, and even they made the final decision to go somewhat in response to a dare that challenged their courage.

Interest in the Yellowstone country had been growing in the Montana mining communities since their founding in the early 1860s. More and more information about the great canyon of the Yellowstone River, Yellowstone Lake, and the geysers and hot springs in the region had become available from the Raynolds Expedition of 1860 as well as from Montana prospectors who ventured there and then returned. The expedition led by Walter Washington DeLacy, discussed in chapter 4, explored the country of the upper Snake River and the upper reaches of the Madison River in 1863. The DeLacy outing had particular influence in the mining territories; after returning from his trip DeLacy was commissioned by authorities in Montana to produce a map of the Yellowstone area and surrounding areas, a map that was first published in 1865. Finally, the trip that Father Xavier Kuppens made to the Yellowstone country with Blackfeet guides, as discussed in Chapter 2, brought back still more information about the Yellowstone country, and a chance meeting between Kuppens and men who were important in the Montana gold mining communities disseminated the information on a wide basis. Montana Territory was a large area geographically, especially in those days of horse-powered transportation, but despite limited communication technology it was a small area socially.

Folsom, Cook, and Peterson followed a route that took them through the new town of Bozeman, where they purchased considerable amounts of supplies to take on their journey. This is an example of how much things had changed in a short time—just a few years earlier, there had been no Bozeman and no other place for hundreds of miles where a party of explorers could have found commercially produced supplies. From Bozeman the men traveled over the mountains to the valley of the Yellowstone River, where they laid over at the Bottler brothers' ranch, which was also new. Philip, Frederick, and Henry Bottler had started their ranch in Paradise Valley just the year

Albert Bierstadt may have been the more established artist at the time, but there is no question it was the work of Thomas Moran that was most influential in leading to the creation of Yellowstone National Park. In this scene a group of explorers from the Hayden Survey of 1871 is climbing up the terraces of Mammoth Hot Springs. Perhaps it was painted, or at least the inspiration for the painting happened, at the same time that Moran's compatriot William Henry Jackson shot the black-and-white photograph of Moran posed on Jupiter Terrace at Mammoth Hot Springs (see page 100). THOMAS MORAN, YELLOWSTONE NATIONAL PARK COLLECTION

Henry Wood Elliott was another artist who accompanied the 1871 Hayden Expedition to Yellowstone. Not as well known as Thomas Moran, Elliott was nonetheless an accomplished painter in his own right. This fanciful composition of Yellowstone Lake may have been set near the lake's outlet, just upstream from today's Fishing Bridge—it is known that the Hayden party camped near the outlet during their explorations of the lake. The rendition may be a composite of landscape features that do not exist in reality, but the painting does capture an essential feeling of what early-day travelers often described as "a large blue lake on the very top of a mountain." HENRY WOOD ELLIOTT, WIKIPEDIA COMMONS

before, and largely because of geography their place would become a stopover for most expeditions to the Yellowstone country during the period of official exploration.

From the Bottler brothers' ranch the Folsom-Cook-Peterson Expedition carried on up the Yellowstone, traveling on a well-used trail on the west side of the river, a trail used by prospectors before them and mountain men before that—and by indigenous peoples for 13,000 years before that. Their route took them through the defile that would soon be named Yankee Jim Canyon, on to the mouth of the Gardner River where the town of Gardiner, Montana, stands today, and finally into what would be established as Yellowstone National Park less than three years later. From there the trio passed over Blacktail Plateau, up the Lamar River, and then over the Mirror Plateau to the Grand Canyon of the Yellowstone River. After spending time around the canyon, they moved up the Yellowstone River through what would later be named Hayden Valley and then took special note of the thermal features in the Mud Volcano area. Traveling beyond Mud Volcano, they were especially taken by Yellowstone Lake, which Folsom described as "one of the beautiful places we had found fashioned by the practised [sic] hand of nature, that man had not desecrated." Saddened to be leaving the big blue lake on the day they started their trek over the mountains toward the Firehole Valley, Folsom further described it as an "inland sea, its crystal waves dancing and sparkling as if laughing with joy for their wild freedom. It is a scene of transcendent

beauty which has been viewed by few white men, and we felt glad to have looked upon it before its primeval solitude should be broken by the crowds of pleasure seekers which at no distant day will throng its shores."

After visiting Shoshone Lake and passing through the very difficult country due east of Old Faithful, Folsom, Cook, and Peterson emerged into the Lower Geyser Basin along White Creek just as Great Fountain Geyser began to erupt at sunset. Great Fountain is particularly stunning at that time of day, with the setting sun backlighting and coloring the eruptive column, and the men waved their hats in the air and whooped and hollered in jubilation. The next day they rode up the Firehole Valley at least as far as Midway Geyser Basin, where they took note of the prodigious discharge from Excelsior Geyser, which scientists later would calculate to be as much as 4,500 gallons of 199-degree water per minute. Soon thereafter they departed the area of the future park by

This is another composition that does not reflect reality because all of the pictured events could not have happened simultaneously. But like Henry Wood Elliott's fanciful painting on page 106, it does capture the essence of the rough-and-tumble nature of a tough trip through Yellowstone in the early 1870s. The Upper Geyser Basin is the setting, with geysers erupting on Geyser Hill on the other side of the Firehole River and Old Faithful likewise erupting in the far right distance. ARTIST UNKNOWN, YELLOWSTONE NATIONAL PARK COLLECTION

way of the Madison River valley, making it back home to Helena on October 11.

❦

Without a doubt, the most important result of the Folsom-Cook-Peterson Expedition in terms of the evolution of Yellowstone National Park came about when David Folsom went to work in the office of the surveyor general of Montana Territory. The surveyor happened to be Henry D. Washburn, and it also happened that Walter Washington DeLacy was likewise employed in Washburn's office. DeLacy used information from Folsom to refine his 1865 map of the Yellowstone area, and of course Washburn was inspired by Folsom's Yellowstone tales to the point that he was moved to organize his own expedition to the Yellowstone country the following summer. DeLacy's map, revised with information from the Folsom party, was finished

Mike Bryers painted this scene of explorer Paul LeHardy and an assistant attempting to run the rapids on the Yellowstone River three miles downstream from the outlet of Yellowstone Lake. LeHardy was a member of the 1873 Jones Expedition, which was sent to Yellowstone to investigate possible road routes for an approach from the south. LeHardy's plan was to float a crude raft with his equipment from the Yellowstone Lake outlet to the brink of the Upper Falls of the Yellowstone River. Unaware of what was to be known ever after as LeHardy's Rapids, he and his partner did not see the danger until it was too late. Their raft became lodged on a rock in midstream, but fortunately the water was only two feet deep, so they were able to carry their possessions to shore and then hike the rest of the way to the falls. LeHardy did break a prized shotgun when he tossed it from the river to the shore. MIKE BRYERS, USED WITH PERMISSION

Lt. Gustavus Doane was an officer in the US Army during the latter decades of the nineteenth century. He is best known for commanding troops who escorted several official exploration parties to Yellowstone in the 1870s, but he also commanded his own winter expedition through the park in 1876–77, an expedition that was ill-advised and ill-fated from the start. After crossing Yellowstone in late October and early November, the Doane party descended the Snake River in boats but nearly perished from starvation and exposure before they were rescued by early-day pioneers in Idaho. This painting by Mike Bryers depicts a camp Doane and his party set up on Topping Point, which is the timbered point of land in front of today's Lake Lodge. The painting accurately shows Yellowstone Lake partially iced—the onset of winter in Yellowstone was much earlier in Doane's time than it is in ours. MIKE BRYERS, USED WITH PERMISSION

James Stevenson (left) and Henry Elliott were both members of the Hayden Survey to Yellowstone in 1871. Here they are pictured in the prefabricated boat that the expedition hauled with them for exploring Yellowstone Lake. The location appears to be along the lakeshore near Storm Point and was probably taken on the day that Stevenson and Elliott used the boat on an excursion to Stevenson Island, which was, of course, named at the time for Stevenson. Hayden himself named the island in honor of his assistant, whom he described as "undoubtedly the first white man that ever placed foot upon it." But that belief may have been in error—there is at least one account of mountain men using a raft to access one of the islands in Yellowstone Lake sometime in the 1830s. Another interesting tidbit is that the name on the boat in the photo is wrong—it was apparently written on the negative at a later time by the photographer. WILLIAM HENRY JACKSON, NATIONAL ARCHIVES

in time for Henry Washburn to take it with him on his trip to the Yellowstone country the following summer.

Henry D. Washburn was born in Vermont in 1832 but moved to Indiana early in life. He taught school and did other odd jobs until becoming a lawyer and entering politics in the 1850s. Like most men of fighting age, he was drawn into the Civil War, where he became an officer in the Union Army and distinguished himself with shrewd leadership and personal bravery through the course of many campaigns, ending the war as a brevet major general. Following two terms as a US congressman, he was fortuitously named to the post of surveyor general of Montana in 1869.

By the summer of 1870, exploring Yellowstone had become a high-status endeavor, and accordingly several prominent citizens of Montana Territory attached themselves to what had already become known as the Washburn Expedition or, as it was alternately named, the Washburn-Langford-Doane Expedition. Nathaniel Pitt Langford was one of those prominent Montana citizens, while Lt. Gustavus Cheney Doane was an officer in the US Cavalry stationed at Fort Ellis, Montana, a post that had recently been established on the eastern outskirts of the new town of Bozeman as a screen against Native American tribes, especially the Sioux, who ranged on the great buffalo plains east of town. Doane was placed in charge of the military escort assigned

Artist Thomas Moran drew this sketch in 1871 of photographer William Henry Jackson retrieving a specimen from the rim of one of Yellowstone's thermal features. No doubt Jackson was acting on a completely natural human impulse to collect a keepsake from a memorable time and place, but there is equally no doubt that such collecting in Yellowstone cannot be allowed in today's world, where over 4 million visitors per year pass through the park. THOMAS MORAN

to accompany the Washburn party, an escort that consisted of Doane along with a sergeant and four privates. The rigid social hierarchy of the time is evident in the roster of men who went on the trip, as listed here in descending order of importance in the opinion of Lt. Doane: "General H. D. Washburn, Surveyor General of Montana, Hon. N. P. Langford, Hon. T. C. Everts, Judge C. Hedges of Helena, Saml. T. Hauser, Warren C. Gillette, Benj. C. Stickney, Jr., Walter Trumbull, and Jacob Smith, all of Helena, together with two packers, and two cooks." Notice that the two packers and the two cooks did not even warrant mention by name. Indeed, one of the horse and mule packers was never referred to in any journal from the expedition by anything other than his last name (and that only rarely), while the two black cooks were seldom mentioned and then only by their first names, Nute and Johnny. And on at least one occasion the cooks were referred to in one of the journals as "the Darkys [sic]."

The Washburn Expedition departed Helena on August 17, joining Lieutenant Doane and the other members of the escort as they passed through Bozeman on August 22. The route they followed was substantially similar to the route followed

Frank J. Haynes was a pioneering photographer who first came to Yellowstone in 1881 and started his successful line of Haynes Photo Shops in the park in 1884. His son Jack Ellis Haynes continued the business until the 1960s, when the photo shops were sold to Hamilton Stores, Inc. by Haynes's widow. This photograph shows Frank Haynes in winter garb while on an 1887 winter exploration of the park, an exploration for which Haynes became de facto leader after the man originally in charge was taken ill and could not continue the trip. There were several photographic "firsts" on that 1887 excursion: Among other subjects, Haynes shot the first winter photos ever taken of Old Faithful Geyser, as well as firsts of the Upper Falls, the Lower Falls, and the Grand Canyon of the Yellowstone River. FRANK J. HAYNES, YELLOWSTONE NATIONAL PARK COLLECTION

Nathaniel Pitt Langford, a pioneering businessman in Montana's goldfields, was a member of the 1870 Washburn Expedition that explored Yellowstone. In 1872 he was appointed the first superintendent of the new Yellowstone National Park. As superintendent he faced almost insurmountable obstacles, including no budget for managing the new creation and no money for a salary for himself. He was replaced as superintendent in 1877 and in later years became a historian. He wrote about his experiences exploring Yellowstone with Henry D. Washburn in a 1905 book titled *Diary of the Washburn Expedition to Yellowstone and Firehole in the Year 1870*. YELLOWSTONE NATIONAL PARK COLLECTION

by Folsom, Cook, and Peterson the year before. Partly because the Washburn party had more members and therefore more eyes on the ground, but also because they spent more time in Yellowstone, they were able to make more observations than the Folsom group. The Washburn Expedition also placed considerably more place-names on the landscape, including many of the most recognizable names still in existence on the Yellowstone map today. Mount Washburn, Tower Fall, Hedges Peak, Beehive Geyser, Castle Geyser, and of course Old Faithful Geyser are just some of the iconic names that date back to the Washburn Expedition of 1870.

One of the more noteworthy events of the Washburn sojourn was when one of its members, Truman C. Everts, became lost in the country south of Yellowstone Lake and could not be found for thirty-seven days. Miraculously,

William Henry Jackson took this photograph of the Yellowstone Lake outlet during the Hayden Expedition of 1871, which led directly to the establishment of Yellowstone as a park early the next year. The composition is similar to the painting of Yellowstone by Henry Wood Elliott (see page 106). The photograph is intriguing for another reason—the outlet of Yellowstone Lake looks much the same today. The sandbar in the middle of the frame is still there, and it is possible to recognize some of the same trees, which are still alive today, from the 1871 photo. WILLIAM HENRY JACKSON, YELLOWSTONE NATIONAL PARK COLLECTION

Everts survived starvation, exposure, and serious burns from geothermal vents and his own campfire, but his ineptitude illustrates that he (as well as several others in the group) was selected on the basis of his social status rather than because of his ability to survive and function in the wilderness environment of Yellowstone in 1870. Everts did manage to walk and crawl fifty miles from the area where he became lost all the way to Blacktail Plateau in Yellowstone's northern reaches, where he was finally found on October 16 by two frontiersmen, "Yellowstone Jack" Baronett and George A. Pritchett. They nursed and fed the emaciated Everts, who weighed only eighty to ninety pounds when they found him, and transported him in stages to Bozeman. When Everts fully recuperated and finally made it back to Helena in November, he was greeted by society there as a celebrity and feted with a lavish banquet. His

This is another of Thomas Moran's beautiful and influential paintings, probably based on his tour with the Hayden Survey of 1871. This work shows what Moran called "The Great Blue Spring of the Lower Geyser Basin," what we today call Excelsior Geyser in the Midway Geyser Basin. Midway Bluff is at the far left, while the steam toward the right of the composition is Grand Prismatic Spring. Several members of the expedition and their horses were placed in the scene for scale. THOMAS MORAN, YELLOWSTONE NATIONAL PARK COLLECTION

Signal Point is just south of the better-known Park Point on the east shore of Yellowstone Lake just north of the mouth of the Southeast Arm. A notable feature of Signal Point is the sharp delineation between forest and meadow behind the point that is in perfect alignment with the point itself. Here, in the right background of this Thomas Moran painting, it is possible to see the Promontory, which separates the Southeast Arm from the South Arm of Yellowstone Lake. The snowcapped peaks in the distance are the southern extremities of the Absaroka Range. THOMAS MORAN, YELLOWSTONE NATIONAL PARK COLLECTION

fame also led to an offer to become Yellowstone Park's first superintendent in 1872, an offer he turned down, but he seemed to have no gratitude to Jack Baronett and George Pritchett, the capable pair who had found him and undoubtedly saved his life. Absurdly claiming that he could have made it the rest of the way to the Montana settlements on his own, Everts refused to pay the promised $600 reward for his rescue to Baronett and Pritchett. This and other snubs by Everts later moved Baronett to remark that "he wished he had let the son-of-a-gun roam," although one has to wonder whether a tough character like Baronett really used the firearm analogy or instead might have referred to a female canine. In any event, Everts ended up having a major eminence near Mammoth Hot Springs named for him—Mount Everts— and also had his name locally applied to a thistle on which he purportedly survived during the thirty-seven days he was missing. Everts thistle is a name commonly used in the Yellowstone area for the plant that elsewhere is usually referred to as elk thistle, a plant known to science as *Cirsium scariosum*. The thistle is indeed edible, for bears, elk, and other wildlife as well as for human beings.

The Washburn-Langford-Doane Expedition returned to Helena in late September, although three of the soldiers assigned as their escort stayed behind for another week in Yellowstone to continue the search for Everts. Importantly, members of the expedition almost immediately began to publicize their trip through magazine articles and other venues. Nathaniel P. Langford in particular was well connected, and he soon embarked on a lecture tour that eventually took him to the East Coast, where his talks had special impact in the centers of power located there. Specifically, Langford was connected to Jay Cooke, the famed financier who had assumed an interest in the Northern Pacific Railroad in the summer of 1870. With the route of an as-yet-unbuilt railroad already planned to pass just north of the Yellowstone area, Cooke could see a future in an attraction that would entice carloads of tourists to use his railroad, and Cooke began to finance Langford's lectures as a way of drumming up interest in the area. Frederick V. Hayden attended one of those lectures in Washington, D.C., on January 19, 1871, and excitement engendered by the lecture coupled with tidbits about the Yellowstone country that Hayden had learned from Jim Bridger and others led directly to Hayden's survey of the Yellowstone country the next summer.

~

Ferdinand Vandeveer Hayden was born in Massachusetts in 1829 but grew up primarily in Ohio. He was a gifted and apparently driven individual who was educated first in medicine, but who later developed his abilities as a geologist and paleontologist. He spent much of the 1850s doing surveys of the Nebraska Territory and other areas along the Missouri River, and then, as outlined earlier, spent most of 1859 and 1860 engaged with the Raynolds Expedition. Not long after that detail he was drawn into the Civil War, in which he served as a physician, primarily in the Shenandoah Valley theater, and after which he recommenced his explorations of the American West. In 1869 he led a party that explored the Rocky Mountain Front from Denver south to Santa Fe, and in 1870, while the Washburn party was exploring Yellowstone, Hayden was leading another party tasked with exploring areas in southern Wyoming.

Federal funding for the 1871 Hayden Survey of Yellowstone was granted by Congress in March, and arrangements for the trip began at that time. Hayden recruited a diverse group of specialists for the trip, including botanists, a meteorologist, a zoologist, topographers, and others. Probably most important to the momentum that was developing toward Yellowstone's designation as a national park, he also took along William Henry Jackson, an outstanding photographer, and artists Henry Elliott and Thomas Moran. Railroad financier Jay Cooke had made special manipulations to ensure that Moran was included on the expedition's roster, and the magnificent paintings Moran produced as a result of the trip would do more than anything else to inspire the creation of Yellowstone as a park.

Following the usual approach for official exploration parties, the Hayden Expedition passed through Bozeman, picking up a military escort at neighboring Fort Ellis en route to the Bottler brothers' ranch in Paradise Valley. They established a base camp at the Bottlers' establishment, and then pushed on up the Yellowstone River and entered the area of the present park near Gardiner, Montana, on July 21. They then traveled up the Gardner River and spent two days investigating Mammoth Hot Springs, where ominously they found two men who had already laid a claim to 320 acres near the springs. The Hayden team then passed over Blacktail Plateau, probably along what would later be named the Bannock Indian Trail, and then spent some time around Tower Fall. From there they passed up and over the Washburn Range to the Grand Canyon of the Yellowstone River, where photographer Jackson took the first known photographs of the Upper and Lower Falls. Next they traveled up the Yellowstone River, passing through the grassy valley that now bears Hayden's name, to the outlet of Yellowstone Lake near today's Fishing Bridge. Here the party divided. Because of its larger size, and because so many members of the party were independently capable, they could safely split into smaller groups and thereby explore more country. Among other undertakings, one group assembled a boat, the prefabricated parts of which had been packed to the lake on horses and mules, and then used it to map the outline of the lake and take soundings of its depths.

While the lake detail was so engaged, Hayden and another portion of the party returned to Hayden Valley and proceeded west over Mary Mountain on a trail long used by mountain men and prospectors, and, longer still, by indigenous peoples. The route brought them to upper Nez Perce Creek, known to them as the East Fork of the Firehole, and then to the Lower Geyser Basin. Hayden and the men directly under his command then spent time exploring the great geyser basins along the Firehole River. From there they passed over difficult, heavily timbered country to Shoshone Lake, and from there back to the West Thumb of Yellowstone Lake. Spending more time to thoroughly explore and also to map the big blue lake from high points above its eastern shore, the reunited party finally left the lake via Pelican Creek over the Mirror Plateau, down to the Lamar River, then northwest along the Lamar to where it enters the Yellowstone. There they found a bridge over the Yellowstone that had been built by Yellowstone Jack Baronett in the autumn of 1870 after rescuing the ungrateful Truman Everts and returning him to the Montana settlements. Baronett's bridge has the distinction of being the first

James Everett Stuart was a landscape painter in the decades around the turn of the twentieth century. He specialized in subjects in the Pacific Northwest but also spent time in Yellowstone and produced work on the world's first national park. Beautiful renditions such as this 1887 piece, *Looking Down the Yellowstone Canyon from Point Defiance*, continued to inspire Americans to lend their support to the national park idea even after the days of official exploration had ended and legal designation of Yellowstone as a national park was accomplished. JAMES EVERETT STUART

Old Faithful Geyser is perhaps the most iconic feature in Yellowstone—perhaps the most iconic of any national park. It was named by members of the 1870 Washburn Expedition, sometimes called the Washburn-Langford-Doane Expedition to include two other important members. The party had just broken out of the trees on the edge of the Upper Geyser Basin when Old Faithful erupted, and the explorers later recorded that they whooped and hollered and waved their hats in the air in jubilation at the sight. After spending several days observing the regularity of the geyser, they gave the feature its appropriate name. JEFF HENRY/ROCHE JAUNE PICTURES, INC.

Ferdinand Vandeveer Hayden was a geologist who led several important surveys through Yellowstone. Hayden Valley, in the very center of the park, is named in his honor. The beautiful open meadow is shown here with the Yellowstone River flowing through the frame and the Washburn Range, also named for one of Yellowstone's first official explorers, in the distance. JEFF HENRY/ROCHE JAUNE PICTURES, INC.

Two more place-names dating back to the era of official exploration are Mount Doane, on the left in this photograph, and Mount Stevenson. The mountains are in the Absaroka Range east of Yellowstone Lake and are named for Lt. Gustavus Doane and James Stevenson, members of the 1870 Washburn Expedition and 1871 Hayden Survey, respectively. The photo was taken early on an exceptionally cold winter morning from the summit of Lake Butte. JEFF HENRY/ ROCHE JAUNE PICTURES, INC.

to span the storied Yellowstone River anywhere along its length. From Baronett's bridge, the party followed the Yellowstone River to the Bottler brothers' ranch, and from there back to Bozeman via the Trail Creek and Meadow Creek Trails.

The results of the Hayden Survey were swift. On December 18, 1871, a bill was introduced in the US House of Representatives to designate the area around the headwaters of the Missouri and Yellowstone Rivers as a park. Ferdinand Hayden, Jay Cooke, Nathaniel Langford, and others not only orchestrated the Hayden Survey of the Yellowstone area in the summer of 1871, but they also directly influenced the introduction of the bill and lobbied to have the bill passed. On March 1, 1872, President Ulysses S. Grant signed the bill into law, establishing Yellowstone as the first national park in the world.

Other official exploration parties entered the park in the years following 1871, but their role was to investigate the area with a finer level of detail and to apply more place-names to the map. All those explorations would take place in an already established park.

Another place-name derived from the period of Yellowstone's official exploration is Mount Everts, named for Truman Everts, who was a member of the 1870 Washburn Expedition. Everts famously became lost in the thick forest south of Yellowstone Lake during that excursion and remained lost for thirty-seven days before being rescued by two intrepid frontiersmen just west of today's Tower Junction. The reedy pond in the foreground of the picture is a kettle pond, a remnant of Yellowstone's glaciation period, while the snowcapped peak in the distance is Sheep Mountain, located outside Yellowstone National Park and just north of the town of Gardiner, Montana. JEFF HENRY/ ROCHE JAUNE PICTURES, INC.

This is another influential painting from Yellowstone's earliest days, influential because such beautiful renderings of park scenes accomplished a great deal in developing a supporting constituency for the new creation. This particular painting is by Albert Bierstadt, who was possibly the most famous landscape painter in America at the time, and shows Great Fountain Geyser erupting in the Lower Geyser Basin. Of substantial interest to more contemporary Yellowstone observers is the unmistakable smoke column in the left background of the painting, indicating that a large forest fire was burning and putting up enough smoke and heat to form a cumulus cloud at the head of the column. Interestingly, the fire that Bierstadt presumably saw was burning in the same area that would burn again in 1988's North Fork Fire, approximately 115 years after Bierstadt's visit.
ALBERT BIERSTADT

The original Fishing Bridge was built in 1902 across the Yellowstone River a short distance downstream from where it issues from Yellowstone Lake. The bridge spanned the river at a place where there had once been a ford on a trail used by Native Americans. As can be seen, the bridge became a very popular spot for park anglers.
PHOTO BY FRANK J. HAYNES, YELLOWSTONE NATIONAL PARK COLLECTION

YELLOWSTONE NATIONAL PARK WAS CREATED on Friday, March 1, 1872, when President Ulysses S. Grant signed a bill recently passed by the US Congress that read in part: "[a] tract of land in the Territories of Montana and Wyoming . . . is hereby reserved and withdrawn from settlement, occupancy, or sale under the laws of the United States, and dedicated and set apart as a public park or pleasuring ground for the benefit and enjoyment of the people; and all persons who shall locate, or settle upon, or occupy the same or any part thereof, except as hereinafter provided, shall be considered trespassers and removed there from [*sic*]." Given the conditions that existed in 1872, the most important phrase in that passage was the provision for the removal of land from settlement, and for the removal from the land of any squatters who might have already taken up residence there. It may be recalled that when the Hayden Survey of 1871 reached Mammoth Hot Springs they found two settlers already there, settlers who had claimed 320 acres of land and commenced building improvements on the site. The population of both the nation as a whole and the immediate region around Yellowstone grew rapidly during the 1870s, as did the transportation networks of the country and the region. Those factors coupled with the development-oriented mind-set of the time meant that settlement of the Yellowstone Park area would have begun very shortly after 1872 had the park not been created. Establishing the park might not have been rendered impossible if settlement of the area had occurred first, but it would have been much more difficult, and the resulting park would have been much less pristine.

Chester A. Arthur was only the first of many sitting presidents to visit Yellowstone National Park. This photograph was taken of Arthur and his party in the Upper Geyser Basin on August 24, 1883, and shows the president sitting in the middle of the front row. The others in the group were all important men in their time, including Gen. Philip H. Sheridan, seated immediately to Arthur's right; and Secretary of War Robert Todd Lincoln, who was the son of Abraham and Mary Todd Lincoln, seated just to the president's left. FRANK J. HAYNES, LIBRARY OF CONGRESS

Philetus W. Norris was named the second superintendent of Yellowstone National Park in 1877. Norris evidently had a penchant for naming features after himself—the list of places bearing his name is quite long and includes the structure pictured here. The building was named the Norris Blockhouse, and it was located on the top of Capitol Hill at Mammoth Hot Springs. Architecturally it reflects the frontier nature of the Yellowstone area when the park was created, and writings left by Norris leave no doubt that he had defensibility in mind when he designed and constructed his blockhouse. YELLOWSTONE NATIONAL PARK COLLECTION

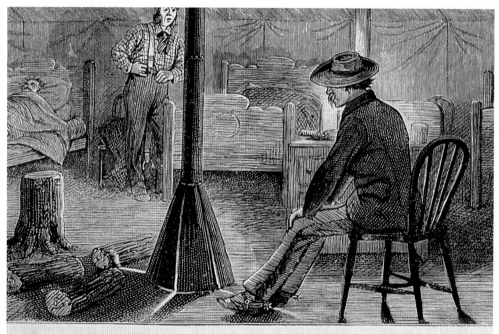

IN A TENT HOTEL, NORRIS BASIN—STRANGE BEDFELLOWS

This woodcut gives some idea of the rough nature of accommodations in the park's early days. It shows the interior of a tent at Norris, complete with a sawed stump that apparently was left on-site for use as a table. The caption suggests that the men pictured may not have been from the same traveling group. YELLOWSTONE NATIONAL PARK COLLECTION

The famous Montana artist Charles M. Russell is known to have made at least one trip to Yellowstone during his life. The stagecoach shown here is typical of the conveyances that began to carry tourists around the park almost as soon as serviceable roads were available. Russell was an extremely sophisticated artist, mostly self-taught, who rarely used backlighting in his compositions. The fact that he did so in this sketch is indicative of how Yellowstone scenes, which commonly include banks of geothermal steam in the background, so readily lend themselves to backlit, silhouetted elements. CHARLES MARION RUSSELL, FROM THE BOOK *CHAPERONING ADRIENNE: A TALE OF YELLOWSTONE NATIONAL PARK*, 1907

The period of early development of Yellowstone might be considered to have begun in 1872, when the park was authorized, through 1920, two years after the end of World War I. To set the evolution of Yellowstone National Park in the context of the nation as a whole, the population of the United States increased from about 38.6 million to 106 million in the fifty years between 1870 and 1920, while the population of the three states from which Yellowstone Park was created grew from less than 45,000 (not counting Native Americans, of course) in 1870 to the almost 1.2 million counted in the census of 1920. The other changes that occurred during that time span, especially within the Yellowstone region, are perhaps even more dramatic than the simple numbers tallying population growth. In the case of Yellowstone, the new park was a wilderness in 1872, known by few Euro-Americans and a place where Native Americans remained largely free to pursue their old ways of living. In 1872 there were no roads and almost no other constructs of Euro-American settlement, and it was still a place where intrepid white hunters were free to trap and shoot game at

Construction of the Old Faithful Inn also necessitated the transport of huge amounts of building materials, which in the winter at that time meant transport by horse-drawn sleighs. Unfortunately, no photographs of the transportation of construction materials to the Old Faithful Inn project are known to exist, but scenes must have been similar to this shot of materials being hauled to the construction of the Canyon Hotel just a few years later. The setting here is Willow Park on the Mammoth–Norris road. YELLOWSTONE NATIONAL PARK COLLECTION

Truman Ward Ingersoll was a photographer from Minnesota who spent substantial amounts of time in Yellowstone around the turn of the twentieth century. In Ingersoll's time it was possible to camp in Yellowstone just about wherever one found an appealing camp-site, and it appears that might have been the case here. Swan Lake is beautifully situated, with Sepulcher Mountain in the right background of this well-composed frame and Electric Peak at the far left. TRUMAN WARD INGERSOLL, BEINECKE LIBRARY, YALE UNIVERSITY

will. But by 1920 Yellowstone had evolved to having a road network recognizable by anyone familiar with the layout of park roads today, and motorized vehicles had replaced horses and wagons on those roads. Not only were the Native Americans long gone, but the park in 1920 also had a full complement of hotels, commercial camps, restaurants, transportation systems, and other services. Much of the park had been electrified, and there was a serviceable telephone system. The National Park Service had been established, replacing the confusion that had reigned in the institutional vacuum present in the park's first fourteen years of existence, and also replacing the US Army's interim presence as protectors of the park from 1886 to 1918. One of the more telling statistics of Yellowstone's growth is that there were 300 non-American Indian park visitors in 1872, but that number swelled to 79,777 visitors in 1920.

For the first dozen years or so of Yellowstone's existence as a park, there was a procession of scientific surveys that greatly increased knowledge of the area. These surveys were in addition to the ones prior to 1872 that had led directly to the establishment of the park. Each successive expedition after park designation added more place-names to the landscape, not only because the country was becoming better known, but also because more intense use required nomenclature down to a finer level of detail—and not just for scientific and geographic exploration. Almost immediately after the park's creation, some of the official expeditions to the area were for the express purpose of surveying for the layout of roads to facilitate access to the newly designated preserve. From the very beginning, proponents of the new creation realized that the continued existence of Yellowstone as a park depended on tourism, and therefore roads had to be constructed to bring visitors to the area and to carry them around the park after their arrival. An interesting sidebar to Yellowstone's history is that the US Army administered Yellowstone from 1886 to 1918, and it was under the army's watch that most initial road construction took place.

For its first fourteen years of existence, Yellowstone National Park mostly existed in title only. The park had no budget, and most of its superintendents did not even live in the park. There was essentially no enforcement presence to protect the park's geologic wonders or its wildlife from the growing numbers of tourists—visitation had grown to about 5,000 visitors annually by 1886—who had an increasingly heavy-handed impact on the park's resources. The defacing of geothermal features by specimen collectors was a rampant problem, as ornate but fragile features that in some cases had taken thousands of years to accrete were torn apart and hauled away in the blink of a geologic eye.

Poaching of the park's wildlife also became an issue as the years went by. It is important to remember that when Yellowstone was created in 1872, protection of its

Another Truman Ward Ingersoll photograph, this one of a jovial crew in a horse-drawn carriage at Castle Geyser. That Ingersoll was dedicated to his craft is evident from the scope of his work—some sources credit him with being the third most important photographer in Yellowstone's early days, behind only William Henry Jackson and Frank J. Haynes. His dedication is also evident from the effort he put into conceiving, arranging, and then executing his creative compositions. Ingersoll himself is in this image, seated in the center of the carriage. TRUMAN WARD INGERSOLL, BEINECKE LIBRARY, YALE UNIVERSITY

Another Truman Ward Ingersoll scene, this one of Excelsior Geyser in eruption sometime during the 1880s. Excelsior was colossal when it erupted, spewing forth a column of boiling water 300 feet in diameter and 300 feet high. It is thought that such forceful eruptions may have damaged the geyser's plumbing system, because the huge eruptions ceased in the 1880s. Other than a few relatively minor periods of eruptive activity since then, Excelsior Geyser's titanic eruptions have been replaced with a continuous discharge—well over 4,000 gallons of hot water flow from the geyser vent every single minute of every single day, all year long. That amounts to approximately 25 percent of the total discharge of the entire Lower Geyser Basin. TRUMAN WARD INGERSOLL, BEINECKE LIBRARY, YALE UNIVERSITY

wildlife was an afterthought, with the legislation creating the park including a provision only against the *wanton* destruction of fish and game—in other words, it was still permissible for individuals to kill wildlife for sustenance while on tour in the park. Another point to remember is that in 1872 Yellowstone was not unique in terms of its wildlife abundance—in 1872 there were still huge numbers of wildlife living in the West, numbers of which are almost uniformly reported to be mind-boggling in the accounts of early-day travelers. A region-wide slaughter of unimaginable scale was already well under way by the time Yellowstone was created as a park, however, and by 1886 almost all the large animals in the park region and elsewhere in the West had been killed off. The slaughter extended into Yellowstone National Park itself, where elk and bison seemed to bear the brunt of the killing. By 1886 the bison in particular were of growing concern, because by then the enormous herds on the Great Plains had been eliminated, bison native to the park had been greatly reduced, and the species was at genuine risk of outright extinction. In a very real sense it was the appearance of the US Army that saved the bison in the park, along with many of its other vulnerable resources. It is also worth emphasizing that by saving Yellowstone's bison, the army made a large contribution toward saving the species as a whole.

The first park lodging facilities and other tourist developments were built under the army's watch as well. Ramshackle structures for overnight accommodation were thrown up in the park's earliest days, but shortly after 1900 they were being replaced by grand hotels like the Old Faithful Inn and the Canyon Hotel. (The oldest hotel still in use, the Lake Yellowstone Hotel, on the north shore of Yellowstone Lake, had already opened for business in 1891.) Notably, most of these hotels and many others were built during the days of horse-powered transportation, so not surprisingly most of them were located about a day's journey apart, with the duration of the journey determined by the speed of horse-drawn wagons along with allowances for stops at park features of interest. Naturally, the major hotels were located near the park's principal attractions, such as the Grand Canyon of the Yellowstone, Old Faithful Geyser, Mammoth Hot Springs, and so on.

Stopovers, often in the form of lunch stations, were frequently built at midpoints between major developments. These were places where tourists could step off the stagecoach tours, dust themselves off, and take a break from the rough ride over the park's bumpy roads while they had a bite to eat. Stagecoach tours through the park, in which visitors stayed in fancy hotels such as the Old Faithful Inn, were expensive and mostly patronized by the well-to-do. Later, a less expensive option for touring Yellowstone evolved in the form of tent camps, which were usually established in the same neighborhoods as the more elaborate hotels. Transportation between the tent camps was still by way of horse-drawn stagecoaches. An even less expensive option was camping on one's own along park roads with one's own horses and other equipment. People touring the park in this independent manner were referred to as "sagebrushers," because that shrub was often present in the sites where they chose to camp.

Other service businesses sprang up in the park's early days, most notably general stores and, in the years after 1915, fuel and service stations for motorized vehicles, which were first allowed into Yellowstone late in the summer of that year. There was a strong family association for many of these early-day park businesses, dynasties that in some cases lasted for generations. This was true for the family of Harry Child, who

Early-day roads in Yellowstone were rough—rough and muddy when wet and rough and dusty when dry. The dusty conditions are illustrated here. PHOTOGRAPHER, DATE, AND LOCATION UNKNOWN, OPEN PARK NETWORK

Oiling was a response to the dusty conditions of early-day roads. This photograph, taken by an unknown photographer, shows a machine spreading oil on the West Entrance Road in 1915. OPEN PARK NETWORK

President Theodore Roosevelt visited Yellowstone in the spring of 1903. Here he and his entourage are pictured as they entered the park's North Entrance in Gardiner, Montana. The president and his entourage were large, and their arrival obviously attracted a lot of interest from locals. The great TR himself is seated on the top of the first coach in the procession. PHOTOGRAPHER UNKNOWN, UNIVERSITY OF CALIFORNIA KEYSTONE MAST COLLECTION

was a pioneer hotelier in Yellowstone largely responsible for the construction of the Old Faithful Inn and the Grand Canyon Hotel, and whose park interests evolved into the Yellowstone Park Company. Child and his descendants were a dominant force in park lodging, along with a considerable portion of the park's transportation business, from the late 1890s until 1966.

The Hamilton Store franchise was even more long-lived—Charles Ashworth Hamilton started his retail business in Yellowstone in 1915, when he bought a rustically picturesque store at Old Faithful. From that one store Hamilton and his heirs built their retail business into a parkwide operation that lasted until the family and the company were forced out of the park in 2002. During their eighty-seven years of operation the Hamilton Stores, or "Ham Stores" as they were colloquially called by visitors and park employees alike, became a Yellowstone institution. So complete was the Yellowstone

monopoly enjoyed by the Yellowstone Park Company and Hamilton Stores that the two companies became shared proprietors of the only other major business concern in the park: the company providing fuel and auto service to a traveling public becoming ever more oriented toward the private automobile.

Railroad companies played a major role in the early history of Yellowstone, going back to the days before the park was even established. Jay Cooke, financier for the Northern Pacific Railroad, had the connections and the financial means to influence passage of the congressional act establishing the park. Cooke's railroad had been granted a right-of-way across southern Montana, a route that passed through the new town of Livingston, only fifty-odd miles north of Yellowstone National Park. The railroad,

Frank J. Haynes shot this scene in front of the Old Faithful Inn on a date not recorded, but it must have been between 1904, when the inn was completed, and 1917, when transportation in Yellowstone switched from horse power to internal combustion engines. This wagon master must have had tremendous skill to control an eight-horse team with three wagons hitched together end to end.
FRANK J. HAYNES, YELLOWSTONE NATIONAL PARK COLLECTION

of course, saw a future business opportunity in transporting tourists to the new attraction, and toward that end began building a spur line toward the park right after their main tracks reached Livingston in 1882. Soon thereafter the railroad began encouraging hotel construction in the park, financing many of Yellowstone's most famous lodging structures, and also had a hand in establishing stagecoach transportation systems to move tourists around the park after they arrived. Tours were often constructed as package deals, with railroad fare combined with overnight lodging and transportation within the park. Such package deals, along with railroad transportation itself, declined through the twentieth century, especially after the Great Depression. This was, of course, due to the advent of the automobile, which allowed

The waters that pool around the rim of Great Fountain Geyser during intervals between eruptions cool to the point where they are not scalding, as evidenced by this happy group of tourists taking the waters around 1908. The visitors were, of course, responding to a natural human impulse; unfortunately, such impulses cannot be indulged by today's visitors to Yellowstone, which number over 4 million per year. PHOTOGRAPHER UNKNOWN, YELLOWSTONE NATIONAL PARK COLLECTION

the American public to travel independently to Yellowstone as well as to other vacation destinations. Train travel to Yellowstone declined precipitously after World War II, to the point where its final demise just after mid-century was hardly noticed.

~

One of the most dramatic events in the early history of Yellowstone occurred just five years after creation of the park. In the summer of 1877 the Nez Perce fled through the park after being displaced from their homeland in western Idaho and eastern Oregon and Washington by encroaching settlers. Pursued by the US Army, the Nez Perce came into conflict with a number of tourists who

This was another activity that was permissible in the park's early days, when standards of safety and institutional oversight were different. It is still possible to descend Uncle Tom's Trail to the foot of the 308-foot Lower Falls, but nowadays the descent is on a set of stairs protected by handrails. The trail is steep, but it is worth the effort to get up close and personal with the thundering falls. PHOTOGRAPHER UNKNOWN, YELLOWSTONE NATIONAL PARK COLLECTION

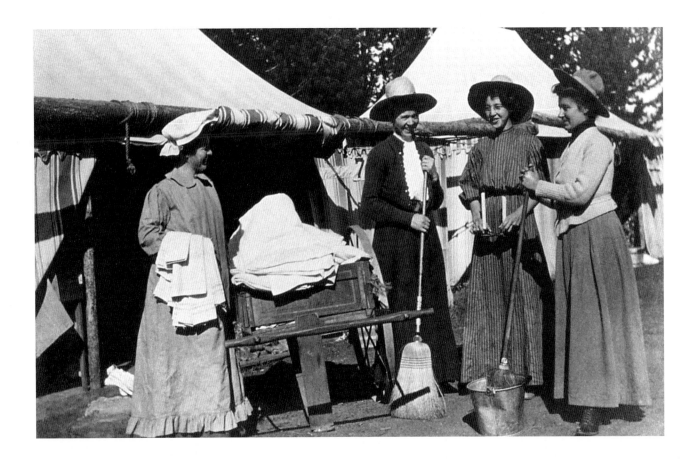

happened to be vacationing in the new park at the same time. They also had skirmishes with some local settlers who had taken up residence in the areas immediately adjoining the park.

The Nez Perce entered Yellowstone along the Madison River, partly following the route of the Bannock Trail that Native Americans (including the Nez Perce) had used to travel to the great buffalo ranges on the plains east of Yellowstone since about 1840, when the shaggy animals disappeared from their home areas west of the Continental Divide. They traveled up the Madison to the Firehole River, then up the Firehole to the stream entering from the east that had been known as the East Fork of the Firehole but was renamed Nez Perce Creek shortly after that tribe's 1877 passage. In the Lower Geyser Basin, near the mouth of Nez Perce Creek, the Nez

The Wylie Camping Company in Yellowstone was formally created in 1883; its purpose was to answer to the needs of middle-class tourists visiting Yellowstone. The company transported visitors around the park in stagecoaches, then put them up in tent lodging at semi-permanent camps in the park. This was a somewhat more affordable option than staying in the park's fancier hotels. Throughout the history of Yellowstone, most park employees have considered their time working in the park to be one of the happiest chapters in their lives. Judging by the expressions on these women's faces, that seems to have been the case when this photograph was snapped in about 1908. PHOTOGRAPHER AND LOCATION UNKNOWN, YELLOWSTONE NATIONAL PARK COLLECTION

172 HECLA OR WHITE DOME GEY. CONE   FIREHOLE GEY. BASIEN.

Perce first encountered an old prospector named John Shively, whom they captured and then held prisoner for most of the next two weeks. Then, in the Lower Geyser Basin, they came across a party of nine tourists from Radersburg, Montana, which was a gold mining boomtown southeast of Helena. The Nez Perce plundered the tourists of their equipment and horses, and shot and wounded two of the party. They also captured three members of the group and held them hostage along with the prospector John Shively.

From Nez Perce Creek the fleeing tribe passed over Mary Mountain to Hayden Valley, and then traveled down Trout Creek to the Yellowstone River at Nez Perce Ford. In Hayden Valley they

In this photograph by Truman Ward Ingersoll taken in the early days of the park, three men have climbed to the top of White Dome Geyser and are looking into its vent. White Dome is located in the Lower Geyser Basin, along Firehole Lake Drive, and still looks much the same as it did when Ingersoll shot this picture. TRUMAN WARD INGERSOLL, BEINECKE LIBRARY, YALE UNIVERSITY

found another group of tourists, this one composed of ten young men from Helena. More violence ensued, and a few unfortunate individuals were killed before the Nez Perce moved on to the east. At about the same time, other detachments of raiding Nez Perce attacked settlers in a nascent development at Mammoth Hot Springs and at a ranch a short distance down the Yellowstone River from today's Gardiner, Montana. There were more casualties and destroyed property in those attacks.

The most celebrated story connected to the 1877 passage of the Nez Perce through Yellowstone was that of George Cowan of the Radersburg party. He was shot three times and left for

The man in this image is standing on Fishing Cone, a hot spring at the edge of Yellowstone Lake at the West Thumb Geyser Basin. He is engaged in an activity that was popular in early-day Yellowstone: fishing from the cone and then dipping a hooked fish into the nearly boiling waters of the spring to cook the fish while it was still on the line. The man in this photograph appears to be black. Given the tenor of the times, he was likely a cook hired by one of the park's business interests, or perhaps was hired to work as a traveling cook by a wealthy party traveling through the park on their own. PHOTOGRAPHER AND DATE UNKNOWN, YELLOWSTONE NATIONAL PARK COLLECTION

This pack train is crossing the original Fishing Bridge, which was built in 1902 and featured a slightly different orientation than the current bridge, which was built in 1937. There are four women at the head of this string of horses, which would seem to indicate that they were the clients and the men riding along behind were their outfitters and guides. If so, this must have been an unusual occurrence for the time, which in all likelihood was before 1917, when the use of horses for transportation over Yellowstone's roads came to an end. PHOTOGRAPHER AND EXACT DATE UNKNOWN, OPEN PARK NETWORK

The US Army arrived in Yellowstone in 1886 and ended up staying until 1918. The arrangement worked well for protecting the park and its resources, much better than the vacuum in management and enforcement that existed before the army showed up. In addition to protective functions, soldiers also provided interpretive information to tourists, as shown in this photograph from about 1903, in which a military man is explaining the operation of Giant Geyser to an interested visitor. PHOTOGRAPHER UNKNOWN, YELLOWSTONE NATIONAL PARK COLLECTION

dead. But Cowan was not dead, and he managed to crawl from where he had been shot to the mouth of Nez Perce Creek, a distance of about nine miles. There he suffered yet another misadventure when he fell into a campfire and was badly burned before he was found by a military man who offered assistance and started him on his way back to the settlements in southern Montana. But Cowan's trials and tribulations were not over. First, the wagon in which he was riding en route to Bozeman wrecked, and after he finally reached civilization in Bozeman, he either was dumped from the stretcher on which he was being carried or suffered further injury when the bed in which he was convalescing collapsed, the exact details of this latter part of the

Another photograph from the period of army stewardship of Yellowstone shows the Old Faithful Soldier Station, which was located in a loop of the Firehole River on the flat in front of today's Old Faithful Lower Store and the Old Faithful Lower fuel station. The perspective of the photograph shows that it was shot a short distance upstream from Castle Geyser, and the steaming hillside in the background is Geyser Hill in the Upper Geyser Basin. The largest steam column in the center appears to be Giantess Geyser in eruption. PHOTOGRAPHER UNKNOWN, YELLOW-STONE NATIONAL PARK COLLECTION

story depending on the source. But Cowan still didn't die, and in fact he lived until 1926, when he was eighty-four years old. He also had a tributary of Nez Perce Creek named for him—Cowan Creek flows through Cowan Meadow on its way to the larger creek named for the tribe that shot George Cowan.

Another similar but much less well-known conflict took place in Yellowstone the year after the Nez Perce fled through the park. The Bannocks had fled their reservation at Fort Hall in eastern Idaho in 1878 for many of the same reasons that the Nez Perce had left their homeland in western Idaho and eastern Washington and Oregon in 1877. After passing through Yellowstone Park without any notable events, they were overtaken by Gen. Nelson A. Miles with thirty-five soldiers and seventy-five Crow

Frederic Remington was a famous artist of the American West who lived from 1861 until 1909. He had a particular affinity for soldiers stationed in the West, and those twin interests led him to create a fair body of work depicting cavalrymen on duty in Yellowstone. This sketch shows a mounted patrol in Yellowstone's backcountry, possibly near the mouth of Violet Creek where it flows into Alum Creek in Hayden Valley. During its tenure in Yellowstone, the US Army protected the park from poachers and others who desired to exploit natural resources to the detriment of the preserve. Their presence was especially crucial in protecting the nation's last wild herd of bison, and many are the stories of heroic efforts made by the soldiers on their often extended patrols. METROPOLITAN MUSEUM OF ART

Because of the severity of Yellowstone winters, explorations of the park during the cold season lagged behind those made during the summer. This man is inexplicably walking on snowshoes while shouldering his cross-country skis—inexplicable because skis are a much easier and more efficient means of locomotion in most snow conditions. This shot was taken on Swan Lake Flat with Bunsen Peak in the distance and demonstrates the kind of effort Truman Ward Ingersoll made in pursuit of his early-day photography, as it must have been an arduous tote for Ingersoll to lug his photography gear to the site. TRUMAN WARD INGERSOLL, BEINECKE LIBRARY, YALE UNIVERSITY

By the late nineteenth century the immense herds of bison that had lived in North America just a few decades earlier were gone, and the species as a whole was perilously close to outright extinction. Yellowstone was the last place in the United States, and is the only place today, where wild bison have persisted from prehistoric times to the present. In addition to the protection offered by the establishment of Yellowstone as a park, reasons for the survival of Yellowstone bison include remoteness, a harsh winter climate, and the fact that Yellowstone is largely forested—the tree cover offered concealment in contrast to the open plains where most bison originally lived. This photograph is illustrative of how bison survived in out-of-the-way openings in Yellowstone's forested habitats. JEFF HENRY/ROCHE JAUNE PICTURES, INC.

By 1902 soldiers conducting an annual winter survey of Yellowstone bison could find only twenty-three individuals. With the wild herd that small, it was decided that the best way to ensure the species' survival in the park was to start a captive herd that could be closely guarded against poachers. Toward that end, C. J. Jones, aka Buffalo Jones, and scout Peter Holt were dispatched to capture bison calves from the wild herd to use as seed stock to begin the guarded herd. Jones and Holt evidently skied all the way from park headquarters at Mammoth Hot Springs to Pelican Valley, where they captured two calves while somehow avoiding the protective wrath of their mothers, lashed the calves to toboggans, and then skied them all the way back to Mammoth. PHOTOGRAPHER UNKNOWN, OPEN PARK NETWORK

Buffalo Jones with, evidently, the two bison calves he and Peter Holt captured earlier in 1902 in Pelican Valley. The calves were apparently suckled by a domestic milk cow, which in the longer scope of Yellowstone history is ironic. It is quite likely that Yellowstone's bison contracted the disease brucellosis from domestic bovines, but it is that disease and the perceived risk of its transmission to herds of domestic livestock that lead to the slaughter of many of the park's bison when they migrate into lower elevations of Montana to escape wintry weather in Yellowstone's high country. PHOTOGRAPHER UNKNOWN, OPEN PARK NETWORK

mercenaries. Miles's detachment attacked the Bannocks not far east of Yellowstone's eastern boundary, killed eleven of them, and then shepherded the survivors back to the Fort Hall Reservation, near today's Pocatello, Idaho.

The flight through Yellowstone by the Nez Perce in 1877 and the Bannocks in 1878 undoubtedly contributed to the fabrication of the myth that Native Americans were superstitiously afraid of the park's geysers and other geothermal manifestations; if tourists were going to be attracted to the new park—and they had to be if the park was going to survive—any lingering fears of danger from Native Americans had to be put to rest.

～

Quite clearly, Yellowstone National Park was created primarily to protect its geothermal wonders, and secondarily to protect its colorful Grand Canyon and the stupendous waterfalls on the

Mattie Culver was the wife of winterkeeper Ellery C. Culver at the Marshall Hotel on the mouth of Nez Perce Creek during the winter of 1888–89, and her story is one of the saddest in Yellowstone's history. Mattie had been diagnosed with tuberculosis prior to arriving in Yellowstone, and that's what killed her on March 2, 1889. She left behind not only her husband but also their infant daughter, Theda. Ellery, in his isolation, initially was unable to gouge a grave for his wife in the hard-frozen ground, so he had to place her body in two sawed-off barrels connected end to end to protect it from scavenging animals until some of Yellowstone's guardian soldiers arrived to help him dig a grave. This painting by Mike Bryers of West Yellowstone, Montana, illustrates the poignant scene at Mattie's burial. Her grave can still be seen adjacent to the Nez Perce picnic area near the junction of Grand Loop Road with the north end of Fountain Flats Drive. MIKE BRYERS, USED WITH PERMISSION

This greenhouse was situated in the Myriad Group of geothermal features just southwest of the Old Faithful Inn and directly behind the Old Faithful Lower Store and the Old Faithful Lower Yellowstone Park Service Station. Heated and irrigated with geothermal water, it was used by Old Faithful winterkeepers to produce fresh vegetables during long Yellowstone winters. The woman peering out the door in this October 1917 photo is unknown, but she may have been Mrs. Musser, wife of the Old Faithful Inn winterkeeper at the time. OPEN PARK NETWORK

The interior of the greenhouse shown in the previous photograph. Fern Barnard, wife of Old Faithful Inn winterkeeper Barney Barnard, can be seen at the far end of the building. The fresh greens produced in the Old Faithful greenhouse must have been a welcome addition to winter larder for snowbound caretakers. One woman who spent the winter of 1922–23 as a tutor for the winterkeeper's sons at Old Faithful described the produce as "a taste of California." OPEN PARK NETWORK

"FOR THE BENEFIT AND ENJOYMENT OF THE PEOPLE"

Yellowstone River. Wildlife that happened to inhabit the area enclosed by the park boundaries was thrown in with the deal. But it's also true that even before the park was created, a slaughter of almost incomprehensible proportions had already begun in the American West. The best-known slaughter of wildlife is, of course, the decimation of the American bison. Their numbers declined from an estimated 30 to 60 million before Euro-American western expansion to less than 1,000 by 1900. The bison slaughter is best known, but animals of almost all other species were subjected to similar carnage. In the great wildlife holocaust of the mid- to late nineteenth century, most animals were killed for their hides or skins, but there was

Legendary Yellowstone photographer Frank J. Haynes shot this picture of a horse-drawn carriage passing through the Roosevelt Arch in Gardiner, Montana. The arch was built in 1903 and famously was dedicated by President Theodore Roosevelt himself when he made a visit to Yellowstone in the spring of that year. FRANK J. HAYNES, YELLOWSTONE NATIONAL PARK COLLECTION

also a great deal of excessive sport hunting, and more than that, a substantial amount of killing just for the sake of killing, which stemmed from some deep-seated, mysterious, and perverse impulse.

Of course, hunting by humans had been a part of life in Yellowstone for a long time before 1872, going all the way back to the first people who showed up here around 13,000 years ago. But that had always been subsistence hunting, not sport hunting, or commercial hunting, both of which had insatiable appetites. That such hunting had begun inside what became Yellowstone even before it was designated a park in 1872 is apparent in a letter written by Lt. Gustavus Doane, who was a major player in the official explorations of the park area. In 1875 he wrote that "the terrible slaughter . . . has been going on

In the park's early days, roads became very muddy during periods of wet weather. Usually more of a problem in spring, apparently there had been some autumn rains, or perhaps a snowfall that had melted, just prior to this photo being snapped in September 1912. OPEN PARK NETWORK

since the fall of 1871 [emphasis added]." The killing of wildlife in Yellowstone not only continued after Doane's report on what was happening in 1871, it also intensified as thousands upon thousands of elk, deer, pronghorn antelope, and other ungulates were killed for their hides both inside and immediately outside park boundaries. By the mid-1880s the numbers of these and other species were greatly reduced, and in particular bison populations within the park had fallen to alarmingly low levels. Surveys by US Army troops who came to protect Yellowstone in 1886 recorded declining numbers of the iconic animals until 1902, when the count bottomed out at twenty-three (although the individuals arriving at that count admitted there were probably a few other bison present in the park that they had not seen).

The steamboat *Zillah* belonged to E. C. Waters, who founded the Yellowstone Lake Boat Company in 1891. The business was apparently successful, but Waters himself was unscrupulous and difficult, so he lost his business and was banned from the park in 1907. In the words of the press statement released by the park superintendent at the time, he was guilty of "having rendered himself obnoxious during the season of 1907 [and] is debarred from the park and will not be allowed to return."
YELLOWSTONE NATIONAL PARK COLLECTION

Predators were not exempt from the slaughter, either. Many wolves, coyotes, bears, and mountain lions were shot outright. Worse yet, hunters often spiked the carcasses of ungulates they had killed with strychnine, which poisoned any carnivores that might feed on the dead animal, condemning them to painful, protracted deaths, after which they were, in turn, skinned by the hunters. Poisoning of carcasses was, of course, non-discriminating, so many non-targeted species, like scavenging birds (eagles, magpies, ravens), were also killed.

Park officials recognized and then responded to the profligate killing of Yellowstone wildlife by passing a law in 1883 that prohibited *all* taking of animals within the park. The law was only marginally effective, however, mostly because of lack of enforcement in the new park, and the poaching

Specimen coating was a popular pastime at Mammoth Hot Springs during the early days of the park. Water from the springs carries with it dissolved limestone, which is deposited on an object much more quickly than the silica-laden geothermal waters in most of the springs in the park. Many entrepreneurs took advantage of this characteristic to coat all manner of objects—horseshoes, chinaware, bottles, drinking vessels, and much, much more—for sale as mementos to Yellowstone tourists. TRUMAN WARD INGERSOLL, BEINECKE LIBRARY, YALE UNIVERSITY

Feeding rubbish to Yellowstone bears seems to have begun shortly after the establishment of visitor services in the park. The spectacle was popular with tourists, but it was not healthy for the animals to be diverted from a natural diet to such artificial foods. It's only one photograph, but the bear pictured here (probably at Canyon in the 1920s) looks to be obese to an unhealthy degree, likely the result of eating a high-calorie diet without having to make much effort to obtain it.
OPEN PARK NETWORK

Another bear-feeding photograph, this one also was probably taken at Canyon in the park's early days. The location appears to be on the slopes behind the site of the Canyon Hotel, which, if so, would place it in the same area as the previous photograph.
FRANK J. HAYNES, YELLOWSTONE NATIONAL PARK COLLECTION

This photograph bears a notation in its lower left corner that reads in part: "WILD ANIMALS ARE TAME IN YELLOWSTONE PARK NORTHERN PACIFIC." It behooved park businesses in the early days to promote the belief that Yellowstone's animals were "tame" as opposed to "wild" for at least two reasons: One was that tameness guaranteed that visitors would have the chance to see them, and the second was that they posed no danger. OPEN PARK NETWORK

As a largely unexploited area, Yellowstone's resources seemed limitless to early-day tourists and administrators. Harry Child (left), early-day hotelier in Yellowstone, and park superintendent Capt. George Anderson (right) show off a profligate catch of cutthroat trout taken from Yellowstone Lake in this 1894 photo. The unidentified man behind the fish rack is dressed as a gentleman, so he probably was not a guide or other low-level lake-area employee. Perhaps he was the manager of Child's Lake Yellowstone Hotel, which had opened for business just three years before this picture was taken. HARRY CHILD III COLLECTION, USED WITH PERMISSION

Henry Klamer reputedly built this store in 1897, although some refurbishment work done in recent years unearthed a foundation stone engraved with the year 1896. Whatever the original date, Klamer operated the store until his death in 1914, after which his wife, Mary (born Mary Rosetta Henderson), and her brother Walter Henderson ran the business until the 1915 season. That year Mary sold the property to Charles A. Hamilton, who in turn used it to begin his Hamilton Store dynasty, a dynasty that ran until January 1, 2003. Note the sign over the doorway on the left that reads "Klamer Store." OPEN PARK NETWORK

A different view of the same general store shown in the previous picture. The date of this picture is September 1917, and a close look will reveal that the sign above the doorway on the east wing of the store now reads "Hamilton's Curio Store." The two men standing on the footbridge over Myriad Creek outside the doorway are not identified, but the figure on the left may be Charles A. Hamilton himself. OPEN PARK NETWORK

situation in Yellowstone was one of the primary motivations for bringing in the army to serve a protective function in 1886. The army was effective in protecting the park, and many are the stories of epic efforts on the part of Yellowstone troopers in their patrols against and their arrests of poachers. The soldiers' exertions were in large part responsible for saving the Yellowstone bison, a population that has the profound distinction of being the only herd of wild bison to survive from prehistoric times right up until the present anywhere in the United States.

The laws and enforcement measures put in place to save Yellowstone's wildlife were so successful, especially after the passage of the Lacey Act in 1900, that shortly after the

turn of the century an opposite problem began to develop—an *overabundance* of wildlife, at least of some species. Problems associated with population increases of species like elk were exacerbated by predator control programs that entirely eliminated native wolves and greatly curtailed populations of other carnivores like mountain lions. In a program that seems peculiar from today's perspective, park management also initiated supplemental feeding of ungulates at the same time they were killing off predators. Between successful anti-poaching measures and the elimination of predators, along with the supplemental feeding programs, the park soon found itself with too many ungulates on hand. The response was to institute herd reduction programs to keep the numbers of herbivores in check. This was the case first with elk and then, at a somewhat later time, for bison as well. The elk surplus became so great that between outright killing of the animals within the park and the capture of live animals for shipment elsewhere to restore eradicated herds in

Despite their growing popularity outside the park, Yellowstone continued to prohibit motorized vehicles for the first years of the twentieth century. That changed in August 1915, when conveyances powered by internal combustion engines were finally allowed. For the rest of that summer and all of the 1916 season, both horse-powered and motorized vehicles were allowed on park roads, but the experiment in sharing did not work well—horses were spooked by the new contraptions—so when the 1917 season opened, only motorized vehicles were allowed on park roads. No date for this photograph was recorded, but it must have been either late in the summer of 1915 or sometime during the 1916 season. The location is near the top of Soap Hill just down from Mammoth Hot Springs, and the scene of the wagon towing the car seems to be an illustration of the unreliability of automobiles at the time. YELLOWSTONE NATIONAL PARK COLLECTION

AUTOMOBILE SCHEDULES, YELLOWSTONE NATIONAL PARK.

DEPARTMENT OF THE INTERIOR.
FRANKLIN K. LANE, Secretary.

EFFECTIVE JUNE 15, 1916.

[Schedule broadsheet with regulations for automobiles in Yellowstone National Park, including sections on stopping over, speeds, horns, teams, and reduced engine power, followed by detailed timetables for routes between Gardiner, Norris, West Entrance, Canyon, Fountain Hotel, Thumb, Lake Hotel, Tower Falls, and Mammoth Hot Springs under Schedule A and Schedule B.]

Park officials came up with these regulations and timetables in an apparent effort to accommodate automobiles in Yellowstone while still protecting horse-drawn wagons and their occupants. In this particular year it seems that automobiles were bearing most of the restrictions, but very shortly thereafter cars would rise to ascendancy and horse-powered conveyances on park roads would become a thing of the past. YELLOWSTONE NATIONAL PARK COLLECTION

other parts of the country, the park removed an average of several thousand elk per winter, which was the season when most herd reduction work took place.

Also in the interest of wildlife, several boundary changes were made to the outline of Yellowstone in the park's early days. Additions to the park, especially along its northern boundary near Gardiner, Montana, were made to add viable winter range. Almost all of Yellowstone is high country—good summer range but too cold and snowy to sustain grazers in the winter. The land acquisitions near Gardiner and in the northwestern corner of the park along the Gallatin River were relatively low in elevation and were made in an effort to bring more balance to the Yellowstone range equation.

CHAPTER 7

BETWEEN THE WARS

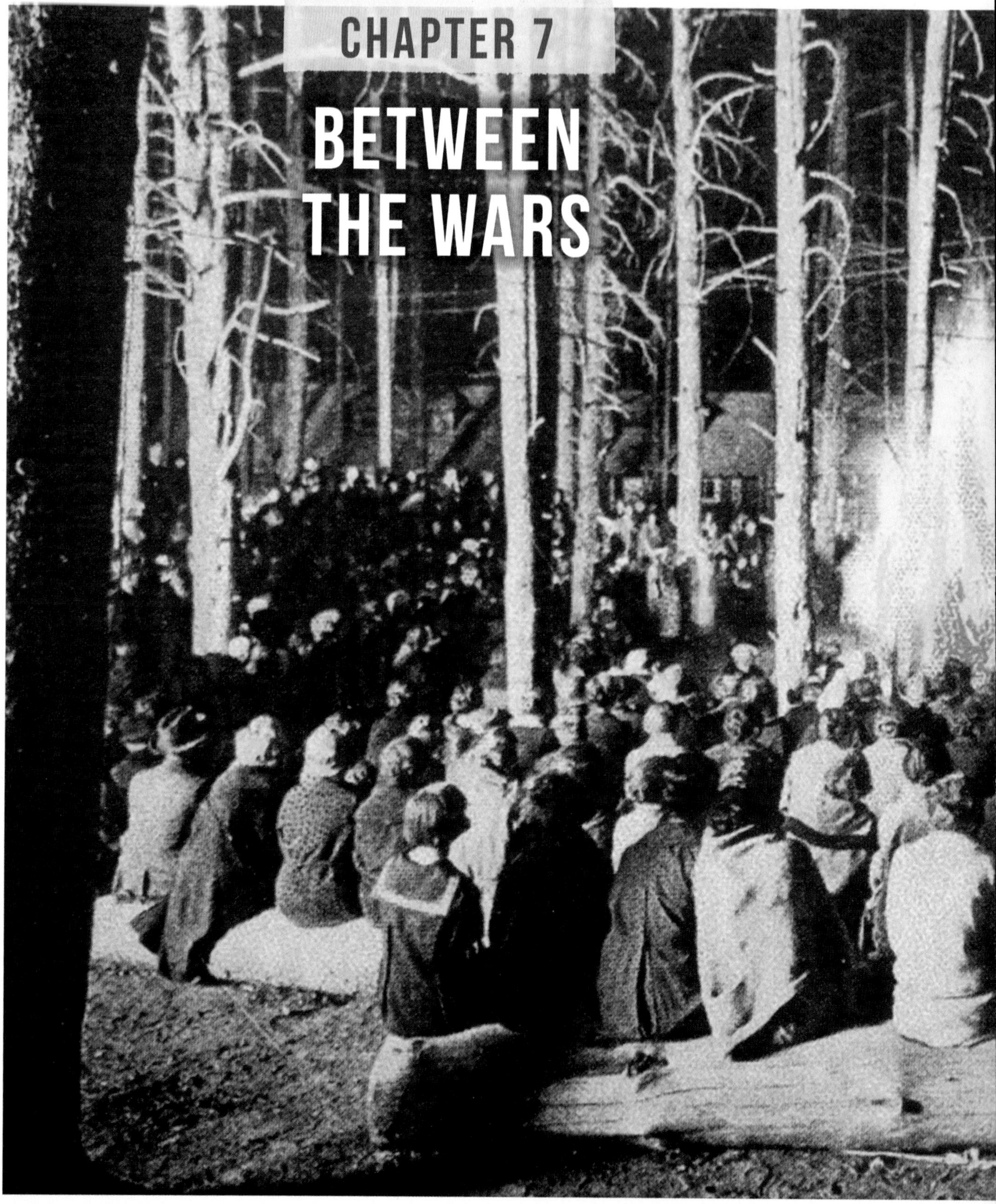

Yellowstone employees often put on evening programs for guests staying in the park's hotels and camps. "Savages," as the employees were called in the parlance of the time and place, would sing songs and act in short skits for the entertainment of visitors, and the performances were usually done around a roaring bonfire such as the one pictured here. That Yellowstone evenings

were chilly in those days is clear from the people sitting in close proximity to the large fire and the heavy clothing most of them were wearing. FRANK J. HAYNES, YELLOWSTONE NATIONAL PARK COLLECTION

THE NATIONAL PARK SERVICE WAS CREATED on August 25, 1916, when the so-called Organic Act was signed into law. The act mandated that the new agency was to manage and promote federal areas "known as national parks, monuments, and reservations . . . to conserve the scenery and the natural and historic objects and the wild life therein and to provide for the enjoyment of the same in such manner and by such means as will leave them unimpaired for the enjoyment of future generations." Of course, it was this legislative act that led to the National Park Service we know today, with its recognizable divisions of law enforcement, interpretation and education, maintenance, research, and so on.

Yellowstone had been moving in the direction of evacuating its US Army overseers and moving toward a return of civilian authority for several years before 1916. When the army first assumed control of Yellowstone in 1886, and for many years thereafter, many of the troopers assigned were not suited for duty in the park—only some had the necessary skills and interests to patrol and manage the park, and to cope with the isolation that came with living in such a remote area. But as time went on, various programs evolved that recruited a few well-suited individuals from army ranks to serve as scouts and other positions in the park, with most such people signing up with the park upon completion of their terms of enlistment in the army. Others living and working in the Yellowstone area who had similar interests and abilities were also hired for jobs such as scouts and gamekeepers, and even before 1916 some of these individuals had come to be called "rangers."

No record of this incident on the South Entrance Road can be found, but based on what can be seen in this photo the story must have been epic. One question that pops into mind is why so many motor vehicles would be attempting to enter through Yellowstone's South Entrance, which is known for prodigious amounts of snow, so early in the season. The man with eyeglasses mounted on one of the draft horses may be Sam Woodring, who was chief ranger of Yellowstone National Park at the time. YELLOWSTONE NATIONAL PARK COLLECTION

By the 1920s Yellowstone's road system had been laid out along lines very similar to those of today. Other improvements had been made as well, but conditions and vehicles were still primitive. This shot was taken in Hayden Valley near Sulphur Spring Creek. PHOTOGRAPHER AND DATE UNKNOWN, OPEN PARK NETWORK

The US Army began winter ski patrols during their tenure in Yellowstone, and the park rangers who followed the troopers continued with the program to protect park wildlife from poachers and to monitor other park resources. These rangers apparently were just beginning their tour as they crouched for a break on a windblown and snow-free point above Africa Lake, which is only three or four miles out from their start at park headquarters at Mammoth Hot Springs. PHOTOGRAPHER UNKNOWN, OPEN PARK NETWORK

Winter transportation has long been a challenge in Yellowstone's deep-snow environment. This vehicle was one attempted answer to the problem of designing a motorized vehicle that could make its way through the snow. It was called the screw drum, or the screw tractor, and its twin drums rotated to auger their way through the snow to propel the vehicle. The novel contraption, which evidently was not in service for long, reportedly hauled mail and other goods from the Gardiner-Mammoth area to Cooke City outside Yellowstone's Northeast Entrance. The screw tractor is pictured here in front of the Buffalo Ranch along Rose Creek in Lamar Valley. LESLIE J. QUINN COLLECTION, USED WITH PERMISSION

Yellowstone's East Entrance Road descends from Sylvan Pass on the crest of the Absaroka Range into Middle Creek. So steep is the descent, and so narrow is the cleft in the mountains through which the road passes, that early-day engineers came up with this clever engineering design to lessen the grade on the road. ASAHEL CURTIS, YELLOWSTONE NATIONAL PARK COLLECTION

The fire lookout atop Mount Washburn, shown in this August 27, 1930, photograph, was built in 1921 and then replaced in 1940 by the structure that stands there today. Mount Washburn is located near the geographic center of Yellowstone National Park, and the view from the summit takes in almost the entire park along with a great deal of country outside its borders. The Yellowstone Park Company continued to run tour buses to the top of Mount Washburn into the 1970s—drivers must have been very mindful of downshifting to low gear for the descent. PHOTOGRAPHER UNKNOWN, OPEN PARK NETWORK

The army contingent assigned to safeguard Yellowstone pulled out shortly after the passage of the park service Organic Act, but because of political jockeying—local businesses profited from the presence of troops occupying Yellowstone and did not want to see them removed—the soldiers returned to the park after an absence of about eight months. The civilian force that had replaced them, amounting to about fifty rangers, was disbanded upon the soldiers' return. The soldiers who came to guard Yellowstone in the summer of 1917 tended to be even less of a match for park duty than troops of earlier times. The United States had entered World War I in April 1917, and it is generally thought that the best troops in the army were sent to the war in Europe, leaving lesser-quality individuals to take care of Yellowstone. Fortunately, the army's stay in Yellowstone this time was brief—the troops pulled out of the park for the last time in the fall of 1918.

The years immediately before and during the Great War were a time of turmoil in Yellowstone.

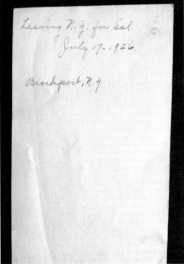

Leaving N.Y. for Cal.
July 17. 1926.

Brockport, N.Y.

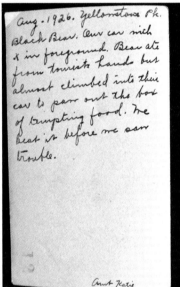

Aug. 1926. Yellowstone Pk.
Black Bear. Our car with
x in foreground. Bear ate
from tourists hands but
almost climbed into their
car to paw out the box
of tempting food. We
beat it before we saw
trouble.

Aunt Katie

These four images consist of two photographs shot by a family named Bryant who traveled from upstate New York through Yellowstone in the summer of 1926. The reverse sides of the photographs are paired with the images to display the notations on the back. Many of the details of the family and their trip, other than those included here, have been lost, but it is known that the family traveled through Yellowstone on a trip from western New York State to California. These images and notes are representative of the great American road trip to Yellowstone Park that has been experienced by millions and millions of Americans over the course of a century and a half.
JEAN BELINDA RICCI FAMILY ARCHIVES, USED WITH PERMISSION

This scene of a bear jam, which may be along the Grand Loop Road just north of Fishing Bridge Junction, would have been typical of the mid-1920s, and for many years before and after that time.
JEAN BELINDA RICCI FAMILY ARCHIVES, USED WITH PERMISSION

Feeding garbage to bears was a favorite spectator sport that began almost as soon as the first hotels opened for business and food service operations started generating waste. Bear feeding for the entertainment of tourists continued for many decades, up until the beginning of World War II. This shot appears to have been taken near Old Faithful, at a site that was named the Bears Playground. PHOTOGRAPHER AND DATE UNKNOWN, OPEN PARK NETWORK

In addition to throwing out food waste to attract bears to bleachers where tourists were seated, garbage generally was poorly managed during the park's early days. Here a black bear appears to be trying to upend a trash can that is decidedly not bear proof. The date on the photograph is November 1928, which in that time period was a little late for a bear to still be out foraging for any foods, natural or unnatural. One has to suspect that the easily available rubbish might have been a reason for this animal to delay its hibernation. PHOTOGRAPHER UNKNOWN, OPEN PARK NETWORK

Not only was there worry about the crisis brewing overseas and then the nation's actual entry into the war early in 1917, there was also the move from horse-powered to motorized transportation. The transition from army to civilian control of the park would have been momentous in any event, but the way it occurred—in fits and starts—made it even more upsetting. America's direct involvement in the Great War lasted for nineteen months, impacting the tourist seasons of both 1917 and 1918 with a substantial drop in visitation. And then the deadly flu pandemic of 1918–19 hit particularly hard in Montana, the neighboring state with which Yellowstone has always been most aligned for supplies and services.

Those disruptions were pretty much resolved by 1920, however, and the decade of the Roaring Twenties saw major developments in Yellowstone. Visitation to the park recovered immediately after the November 11, 1918, armistice,

The angle of the light and the condition of the snow suggest that it was late in the spring when these men were toiling to clear the South Entrance Road, a part of the park known for accumulating tremendous amounts of snow. The crew, several of whom are wearing the signature Stetson flat hat of the park service, was probably clearing the last residual drifts from the road before the park opened for visitors in 1927. PHOTOGRAPHER UNKNOWN, OPEN PARK NETWORK

with over 62,000 tourists arriving in 1919. The next season, in 1920, visitation reached a level more than twice that of 1916, the last tourist season before the US entry into the war. The biggest agent of change in Yellowstone during the 1920s was the personal automobile.

For the first few years after private automobiles were allowed into Yellowstone, operators were advised to carry their own fuel, oil, and replacement tires when they toured the park. That began to change when park stores started selling gasoline out of fifty-five-gallon drums for a dollar a gallon—an astronomically high price for the time. Things got better in 1919 when the first dedicated fuel station opened at Mammoth. Soon more filling stations opened around the park, and prices for gasoline came down to the somewhat more reasonable price of forty to

The Fountain Hotel was located in the Lower Geyser Basin, on the east side of the Grand Loop Road and the south side of Fountain Flats. It opened for business in 1891 and then closed forever at the end of the 1916 season. It was an elegant establishment, offering luxury accommodation to those who could afford it and using hot geothermal water to provide some of its amenities. A diagonal line can be seen crossing the white thermal plain between the pool in the foreground and the hotel. The line was a buried pipe that transported hot water from Leather Pool to the hotel, and the line across the thermal plain can still be seen today—even though the Fountain Hotel was removed in 1926. PHOTOGRAPHER UNKNOWN, YELLOWSTONE NATIONAL PARK COLLECTION

For much of Yellowstone's history the presence of bears within developed areas was commonplace, to the point where they were just part of the scenery, and interaction between the animals and humans was considered to be not a big deal. Judging by the expressions of the children and the apparent attitude of the photographer, this moment of two children feeding the young black bear appears to be a casual encounter. PHOTOGRAPHER UNKNOWN, OPEN PARK NETWORK

This promotional still was taken from a 1925 Hollywood movie titled *The Thundering Herd*, which starred Gary Cooper. The actress opposite Cooper in this frame is possibly Maxine Elliott Hicks, who was something of a Hollywood star at the time. A scene in the *The Thundering Herd* featuring a buffalo stampede was filmed in Yellowstone National Park's Lamar Valley, with the stampede staged by the park service for the benefit of the movie production. As far as star Gary Cooper and his role in the movie, the native Montanan had worked as a tour bus driver in Yellowstone just a few years prior to becoming a movie star, although in the case of this particular production, Cooper was probably not on scene for the filming of the stampede in Lamar Valley. PARAMOUNT PICTURES, 1925, PUBLIC DOMAIN

This still photograph depicts the buffalo stampede in Lamar Valley put on by the park service for the Gary Cooper movie described in the previous photo. To lend a little more drama to the scene, the park service apparently brought in some Crow horseback riders in full regalia to participate in the stampede. UNKNOWN PHOTOGRAPHER, OPEN PARK NETWORK

PARAMOUNT PICTURES, 1925, PUBLIC DOMAIN

forty-five cents per gallon, which was still two to three times the national average price for the fuel at the time.

Roads were being improved at the same time, and in the early 1920s Yellowstone began operating a number of public auto campgrounds around the park, offered to travelers free of charge. These campgrounds were soon followed by the construction of rustic cabins, often referred to in Yellowstone as "campers' cabins," with the cabin areas often located next to the existing campgrounds. Cafeterias, also aimed at serving tourists traveling by car, were constructed adjacent to the new cabin areas. So-called lodges were built to serve as registration buildings for tourists seeking to stay in the

The Crows involved in the 1925 buffalo stampede in Lamar Valley were allowed to kill some of the animals, as evidenced by these strips of meat hung on ropes to dry near their camp. The wall tent is in contrast to the tepees used by their forebears, but the strips of meat hung to dry are consistent with the way meat was cured in the old days. The camp in this photograph was located along Rose Creek adjacent to the Lamar Buffalo Ranch, where bison were ranched for decades in a measure to save the herd from extirpation from Yellowstone. PHOTOGRAPHER UNKNOWN, OPEN PARK NETWORK

Beulah Brown was a summer employee in Yellowstone when a family named Musser, who were winterkeepers at Old Faithful, hired her to tutor their three sons through the winter of 1922–23. In her own words, Beulah "jumped at the chance," and so was able to spend that winter living in the winterkeeper cottage behind the Old Faithful Inn. This photo shows Beulah posing with her snowshoes and cross-country skis outside the winterkeeper house. FROM *MY WINTER IN GEYSERLAND* BY BEULAH BROWN, 1923

Barney and Fern Barnard were winterkeepers at Old Faithful, apparently beginning sometime in the late 1920s and extending into the late 1930s or possibly the early 1940s. During that time it was common for bears to den for the winter under hotel properties in Yellowstone, and apparently Fern and Barney had somehow found this bear cub, probably with its mother and possibly some siblings, asleep under the floor of a cabin rented to tourists in the summer. The Barnards also apparently informed park service officials of their find, as there are other photos of the same scene with the chief park naturalist in a similar pose with the little black bear cub. PHOTOGRAPHER UNKNOWN, OPEN PARK NETWORK

Construction began on the Basin Auto Camp Store at Old Faithful—otherwise known as the Upper Hamilton Store at Old Faithful—in 1929 and was completed in 1930, so this February 1931 photograph of a winterkeeper chopping snow from the eaves was taken during the first winter that the structure was complete. The winterkeeper must not have been experienced or aware of conditions, as he is disturbing the snow on the roof while standing directly in the avalanche zone under the eaves (the building has been known to avalanche on a number of occasions). PHOTOGRAPHER UNKNOWN, OPEN PARK NETWORK

Posing in front of Old Faithful Geyser, this winterkeeper, known only as Mr. Bauer, and Ranger Charles Phillips were photographed only a short time before Phillips's tragic death as the result of eating the virulently poisonous water hemlock in a case of mistaken botanical identity. Phillips died on April 11, 1927, after finding green plants growing along a geothermal runoff stream in the Old Faithful area. He and Mr. and Mrs. Bauer ate the greens as a treat after a long winter with no fresh produce. Mr. and Mrs. Bauer did not like the taste and so didn't eat much of the plant. They were greatly sickened but recovered; when they went to check on their friend, they found Ranger Phillips dead on the floor of his quarters. PHOTOGRAPHER UNKNOWN, OPEN PARK NETWORK

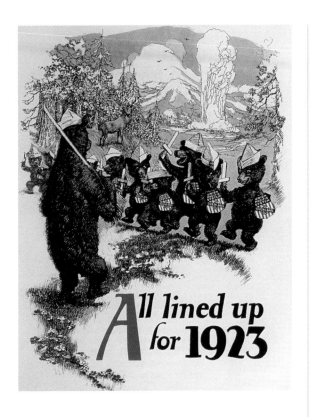

Railroad companies had a stake in the promotion of Yellowstone for many decades after the park's creation. Not only did they profit from transporting passengers to the park, the companies also had substantial investments in park hotels. Posters like this were common, and it was also common to see caricatures of park wildlife as not only harmless but also emasculated to the point of being reduced to a clownish image. UNION PACIFIC RAILROAD, YELLOWSTONE NATIONAL PARK COLLECTION

Always primed to entertain important people in the park, Superintendent Horace Albright apparently arranged for Wyoming governor Nellie Tayloe Ross to attend Yellowstone's spring opening at the West Entrance in this shot from the mid-1920s. Ross was governor of Wyoming for only a short time but went on to a distinguished career that included a twenty- year tenure as director of the US Mint. She lived until 1977, when she was 101 years old. Ranger Frieda Nelson worked in Yellowstone in 1925 and 1926, and also went on to have a long and distinguished life of her own, living until 1978. PHOTOGRAPHER UNKNOWN, YELLOWSTONE NATIONAL PARK COLLECTION

Fish of many different species, including numerous non-natives, were aggressively stocked in park waters in the early days to enhance angling opportunities for visitors. In this 1922 photograph these rangers were stocking fish into the Lamar River near its junction with Soda Butte Creek. As indicated by the lettering on the cans, the fish they were planting came from a fish hatchery near Emigrant, Montana, about thirty-one miles north of Yellowstone's North Entrance. The fish cans were probably loaded on the morning train running through Emigrant at about 9:30 or 10:00, then hauled to Gardiner and placed on trucks for the trip to Lamar. In 1922 the Emigrant hatchery was primarily producing eastern brook trout, so that is likely the species these rangers were dumping into the Lamar at the time the photograph was snapped. PHOTOGRAPHER UNKNOWN, OPEN PARK NETWORK

cabins. The cabins themselves were sparsely furnished, but they were heated with small woodstoves and supplied with enough firewood to warm the chill air of a summer night in Yellowstone's high country.

General stores in the park experienced a growth spurt in the 1920s, also largely because of automobile-borne tourists. Stores were naturally located near the campgrounds and cabin areas, too, and shower houses were built in similarly adjacent locations. One old shower house that still exists today has been converted to an employee dorm for the summer employees of Yellowstone General Stores; it stands just east of the general store at Fishing Bridge along the road to the East Entrance of the park. That particular shower house served the Fishing Bridge Cabin Area, which once comprised several hundred cabins located behind the Fishing Bridge General Store; almost all of those cabins have been removed.

This is a snapshot of the great American pilgrimage to Yellowstone—several generations of family, two vehicles, loads of gear, camping in the great national park. These people were roughing it, as it appears there is new snow on the ground as well as draping the branches in the trees beyond the camp. PHOTOGRAPHER AND LOCATION UNKNOWN, OPEN PARK NETWORK

James McBride was a scout in Yellowstone beginning in 1900, during the time when the US Army protected the park. He may have served as a soldier in the detail occupying Yellowstone before his time as a scout. After the creation of the National Park Service he became a ranger, and then served as the first chief ranger of Yellowstone for a time. McBride was a true frontiersman and apparently had a hard time adjusting to modernization, especially with regard to motor vehicles. Perhaps that's why he was using a motorcycle here, because it was more like a horse than a closed-in automobile. Even the strap securing the boot of the sidecar bears a strong resemblance to a strap on a horse's saddle. PHOTOGRAPHER AND LOCATION UNKNOWN, OPEN PARK NETWORK

Profligacy was common in the early days of the park, when visitors were few and resources abundant. These men and boys were obviously very pleased with their large catch. The location of their take is not recorded, but judging by the presence of the lodgepole pines in the background, it must have been somewhere in the park's higher elevations. PHOTOGRAPHER AND LOCATION UNKNOWN, YELLOWSTONE NATIONAL PARK COLLECTION

Here a park ranger has dipped a handkerchief into Handkerchief Pool in Black Sand Basin. The pool would reputedly clean such an article by way of its heat and its roiling motion, sometimes belching the hanky out of the pool when the cleaning was complete. ASAHEL CURTIS, 1911, HAROLD B. LEE LIBRARY, BRIGHAM YOUNG UNIVERSITY

This store on the north side of Yellowstone Lake, just east of the Lake Yellowstone Hotel, was built in 1922. At some point it was fitted with this canopy-like structure built out of burled lodgepole pine, but exposed to the weather as it was, the structure rotted and apparently collapsed in the early 1950s. PHOTOGRAPHER UNKNOWN, OPEN PARK NETWORK

Gateway communities around the park also benefited and grew as a consequence of the ascendancy of the automobile. West Yellowstone, Montana, at the park's West Entrance, grew up around the railhead of the Oregon Short Line Railroad, which itself was a spur extending from the Union Pacific Railroad's main line in Idaho Falls to Yellowstone's western boundary near the point where the Madison River exits the park. The railroad reached its terminus at the park boundary in the autumn of 1907 and began carrying tourists to the park the next summer, but the town that began to grow around the railhead developed slowly and did not even assume the name "West Yellowstone" on a permanent basis until 1920. After that date "West," as it is usually called by locals, grew more rapidly as tourist shops, fuel stations, hotels, and other services were constructed to cater to growing numbers of Yellowstone visitors, more and more of whom came to the park in their own automobiles. Still, West Yellowstone remained isolated to a great extent for much of the rest of the twentieth century. That was particularly true

In an effort to keep its bison herd propagating and safe from poachers, Yellowstone National Park ranched the animals at the Lamar Buffalo Ranch for many decades in the twentieth century. Part of the program involved producing hay in Lamar Valley to feed the animals. The man in this 1930 photo was using a tractor to plow the native sod, which was then replaced with non-native grasses intended to produce larger crops of hay. PHOTOGRAPHER UNKNOWN, OPEN PARK NETWORK

In this February 15, 1940, photo, caretakers at the Lamar Buffalo Ranch are shown feeding hay most likely produced nearby to the ranched herd of bison. Some of the fencing on the ranch is visible in the foreground. PHOTOGRAPHER UNKNOWN, OPEN PARK NETWORK

in the winter, when the area's legendarily deep snows and severely cold temperatures cut off the town and its few year-round residents from the outside world, leaving them stranded by unplowed highways from the larger towns of the region, which were quite distant even when roads were bare and dry in the summer.

Gardiner, Montana, situated at Yellowstone's North Entrance, also experienced a boom coinciding with the advent of the private car, although the Northern Pacific Railroad had reached its vicinity in 1883, so development had commenced earlier than it had in West Yellowstone. Gardiner always benefited economically from being a supply center to park headquarters, located just five miles up the hill at Mammoth Hot Springs, so its economy in the park's early days was more diversified.

The paired hamlets of Cooke City and Silver Gate, Montana, just outside Yellowstone's Northeast Entrance, largely assumed their present appearance in 1936 upon completion of the Beartooth Highway, which was a remarkable engineering achievement for its time and a highway that has often been described as passing through some of the most beautiful scenery in the world. Cooke City began as a mining town

Elk were not actively ranched as bison were, but because they were protected by Yellowstone's status as a reserve and also by the elimination of most natural predators, they were subject to herd reduction measures. One method was to lure the animals into an enclosure, often baited with hay, after which they would be shot or, in some cases, captured and then transported to augment elk herds elsewhere. PHOTOGRAPHER AND DATE UNKNOWN, OPEN PARK NETWORK

These bull elk have been captured and crated for shipment to Virginia to restore a population of elk that had been extirpated from that state. The location of the photograph may be along Slough Creek, and it further appears that the bulls have had their antlers sawed off, probably to prevent them from injuring each other or their handlers while en route to Virginia. PHOTOGRAPHER AND LOCATION UNKNOWN, OPEN PARK NETWORK

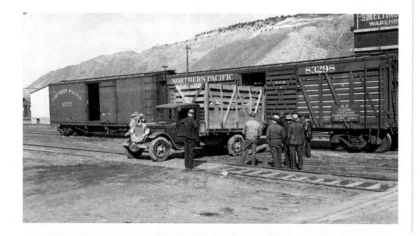

Another shot of the live transport of elk out of Yellowstone as a method of herd reduction, this photograph was taken at the railroad station in Gardiner, Montana, at the park's North Entrance. The elk in the truck in the process of being transferred to the train car may even be part of the same group pictured in the sleighs in the previous photo. PHOTOGRAPHER UNKNOWN, OPEN PARK NETWORK

Park employees sometimes simply shot elk on the range as a way to control the population. That's what apparently happened here along Slough Creek—someone shot these two large bull elk, and draft horses were dragging the carcasses to a slaughter yard where the elk would be butchered. Yellowstone Park most often donated the meat from culled animals to Native American reservations or to charities. PHOTOGRAPHER UNKNOWN, OPEN PARK NETWORK

If these photographs from that year are any indication, 1935 must have been a year of a major elk herd reduction effort. Shown here are elk killed in Yellowstone, the carcasses of which have been trucked to the railhead in Gardiner, Montana, for shipment out on trains. The carcasses are frozen solid from the cold winter weather in the park, which is always in contrast to the much milder conditions usually present in Gardiner. PHOTOGRAPHER UNKNOWN, OPEN PARK NETWORK

in what nineteenth-century prospectors dubbed "The New World Mining District." Euro-American settlement of the town began about 1870, and the town boomed for a time as a mining center. Decline had set in by the time the Beartooth Highway was constructed, however, and the new highway brought traffic that resuscitated the run-down little town. Silver Gate, in turn, did not even exist until the early 1930s, when it was founded to serve tourists visiting Yellowstone Park just one mile to the west, and also to serve the construction project building the Beartooth Highway. Local lore has it that the "service" of the construction project also included "servicing" of the construction workers by prostitutes who supposedly set up shop in Silver Gate, especially in the multi-roomed, still extant Range Rider Hotel.

Yellowstone's South and East Entrances were more distant from any settlement of size, but a number of dude ranches and other services were established just outside both gates in response to the increase of automobile travel. Flagg Ranch, just two miles south of Yellowstone National Park and fortuitously located between Yellowstone and Grand Teton National Parks, was actually founded in 1910, but

Flagg and other guest services in the area profited greatly from increased traffic brought to the area by the automobile. Pahaska Teepee, originally built as a hunting lodge by the famous frontiersman and showman Buffalo Bill Cody, was similarly located just two miles outside Yellowstone's East Entrance. Pahaska Teepee, which means "Long Hair's Lodge" (Buffalo Bill famously wore long golden locks), the name given to it by some of Buffalo Bill's Sioux friends, was only one of several similar lodges/dude ranches that grew up in the vicinity. All experienced a boom with the coming of large numbers of automobile-borne tourists.

In management actions that are decidedly peculiar from today's perspective, the park service in Yellowstone not only killed off what were considered to be excess ungulates, but also carried out aggressive predator control programs at the same time. These coyotes were trapped, killed, and skinned in the Hellroaring Creek area, either by a park service employee or someone skilled as a trapper and contracted by the agency to do the work. PHOTOGRAPHER UNKNOWN, OPEN PARK NETWORK

Standards were different back in the day—cars parking on geyser plains and visitors walking up to the very orifices of geysers are almost beyond comprehension by today's values. This August 2, 1931, photo was taken at Daisy Geyser in the Upper Geyser Basin. PHOTOGRAPHER UNKNOWN, OPEN PARK NETWORK

Park officials often invited regional Native American tribes to Yellowstone on special occasions, such as the spring gate opening at the East Entrance in 1927 in this photograph. Like so many other efforts by the park service in its early days, such events were staged as spectacle for the enjoyment of tourists. In those years the agency felt it was essential to attract visitors to ensure a constituency of supporters for the continued survival of the national park experiment. PHOTOGRAPHER UNKNOWN, OPEN PARK NETWORK

The period between the two world wars was a time of uncertainty regarding Yellowstone's boundaries, with proponents of the park advocating enlargement of its boundaries and development interests outside the park resisting such land additions. As originally created, Yellowstone was a perfect rectangle, and several of the boundary changes proposed by park advocates in the 1920s and 1930s were suggested to conform to hydrologic drainages. Under these proposals some of the boundary adjustments actually sacrificed lands protected under the park's original layout. Most of these proposals succeeded, and a look at a map of today's park boundaries shows that the northern and especially the eastern borders conform to the hydrologic outlines of the landscape, with entire drainages of many watercourses either contained within or excluded from the park. The result is a boundary line that zigs and zags along drainage divides rather than following straight lines of latitude and longitude.

Other land additions were made along the park's northern border during the interim between the wars, most of them west of the town of Gardiner, Montana. Those

This marina and office were located on the north shore of Yellowstone Lake, right in front of the Lake Yellowstone Hotel. The man pointing in the left foreground is presumably an employee, possibly a fishing guide. Like many before his time and many more since, he was pointing out something of interest on the lake. PHOTOGRAPHER UNKNOWN, OPEN PARK NETWORK

Even after horses were no longer used as the principal source of power for traveling over Yellowstone roads, there was still a sense of the romance of the Old West in the park, and this was reflected in the horse rides that continued to be offered to the visiting public. The trail ride saddling up in front of the Old Faithful Inn in 1926 is interestingly juxtaposed with the touring cars loading up directly by the inn. HENRY PEABODY, UNIVERSITY OF CALIFORNIA KEYSTONE COLLECTION

---

lands were low-elevation country, annexed in an attempt to provide more suitable winter range for ungulates that spent summers in Yellowstone's high country. Those additions are clearly seen as jogs in the otherwise straight line of the park's northern boundary. The substantial bulge in the rectangular park boundary in its northwestern corner, along US Highway 191 and near the headwaters of the Gallatin River, was also made in an effort to provide more winter range.

Another, much larger proposal to add to Yellowstone National Park involved a large chunk of land to the south. The goal of park proponents in this area was to provide more security for Yellowstone's migratory elk herd that resided in the high country south of Yellowstone Lake in the summer, and then migrated south to and through Jackson Hole in the autumn en route to more suitable winter range. The proposal to add more land in the Jackson area to Yellowstone was also a move to try to protect the spectacular landscapes in and around the Teton Range. These efforts to add land in the Jackson Hole area to Yellowstone were unsuccessful, but the area did receive national park protection when Grand Teton National Park was created in 1929, with its northern boundary only ten miles south of Yellowstone.

Yellowstone National Park was seriously threatened with the possibility of water development projects within its boundaries through the 1920s and 1930s. Agricultural interests in Idaho longed to take water from the park's southwestern corner, with some of their proposals involving the construction of a dam on the Bechler River. This would have turned beautiful Bechler Meadows into a lake with water levels that fluctuated through the seasons and from year to year, a pattern that would have frequently left unsightly mudflats exposed. An even scarier proposal came from irrigators in Montana, who sought to have a dam built at or near Fishing Bridge in order to raise the level and control the outflow of Yellowstone Lake. Later in the interwar

This August 1933 photograph depicts a "dude" ride in the Old Faithful area. Clearly the picture was composed right in front of Old Faithful Geyser itself, and in another contrast between past and present viewpoints, both the mounted and the pedestrian visitors are much closer to the erupting geyser than today's regulations would allow. PHOTOGRAPHER UNKNOWN, OPEN PARK NETWORK

Herma Albertson first worked in Yellowstone in 1926, as a cabin maid for the concessions company at Old Faithful. She began her park service career that summer as well, working as a naturalist during off time from her day job. She became a full-fledged seasonal naturalist in the summer of 1927 and was photographed two years later in her park service uniform, posing by a stack of shed elk antlers at park headquarters. Shed elk antlers were often used for ornamentation in and around park buildings in Herma's time, as well as before then and for a long time after. PHOTOGRAPHER UNKNOWN, YELLOWSTONE NATIONAL PARK COLLECTION

President Warren Harding and his wife, Florence, visited Yellowstone in the summer of 1923. In this photo the president and first lady apparently had just embarked for points south from Mammoth Hot Springs in the escort of Superintendent Horace Albright and Harry Child, owner of the Yellowstone Park Company. Child no doubt furnished the touring car for the presidential outing, and he must have been appalled when the car developed some sort of mechanical problem just two miles or so out of park headquarters at Mammoth. The car apparently conked out at a pull-out above Africa Lake, with Bunsen Peak in the background. HARRY CHILD III COLLECTION, USED WITH PERMISSION

Another shot of the Hardings' 1923 visit to Yellowstone, this one shot at the very edge of Grand Prismatic Spring with the Twin Buttes in the distance. President Warren Harding died in early August 1923, only one month after his and Florence's visit to the park. PHOTOGRAPHER UNKNOWN, OPEN PARK NETWORK

President Calvin Coolidge also visited Yellowstone, in 1927 with his wife, Grace. Here they are pictured with Superintendent Horace Albright and other members of the president's entourage as they walked up the approach to Roosevelt Lodge. Some members of the group look a little concerned about the black bear family blocking their route, while others look nonchalant and First Lady Grace Coolidge seems downright amused by the scene. YELLOW-STONE NATIONAL PARK COLLECTION

President Franklin Delano Roosevelt and his wife, Eleanor, came to Yellowstone in the autumn of 1937. They are pictured here with Superintendent Edmund B. Rogers in a fancy car at Mud Volcano. YELLOWSTONE NATIONAL PARK COLLECTION

This photograph illustrates the popularity of watching bears at feeding grounds where park rubbish was put out to attract them. The Canyon bear feeding grounds were along Otter Creek, about two and a half miles south of today's Canyon Junction. So many vehicles are parked in this picture that there must have been a considerable traffic jam when the evening's entertainment was over. Most of the bears that came to the Otter Creek feed site were grizzlies. PHOTOGRAPHER UNKNOWN, OPEN PARK NETWORK

An unknown man photographs mule deer at Mammoth in what appears to be late winter conditions with weathered snow. The deer probably had been fed around the housing areas at Mammoth, and so had grown accustomed to human beings. PHOTOGRAPHER UNKNOWN, OPEN PARK NETWORK

The park service apparently kept and housed a pet coyote named Gyp somewhere near the Mammoth Buffalo Corral during the 1920s. In this picture Gyp seems to be focused on an object a short distance in front of his nose. Perhaps it was a morsel of food put out by his admirers, but in any event it is enough of a distraction that he doesn't seem to mind being petted by the woman standing over him. PHOTOGRAPHER UNKNOWN, OPEN PARK NETWORK

period, agriculturalists in both Idaho and Montana collaborated in a renewed effort to have the dam built at Fishing Bridge and the level of Yellowstone Lake raised to the point where some of the lake's water could be pumped through a tunnel to Shoshone Lake or Lewis Lake, where the water could then be dumped into the Snake River system and allowed to flow from there into Idaho. Fortunately, all of these proposals, which would have drastically altered the appearance and character of the park, were defeated by Yellowstone defenders.

~

Another fascinating, albeit little known, chapter of Yellowstone history during this time period is the story of Prohibition in the park. The Volstead Act prohibiting the production, importation, and sale of alcoholic beverages was ratified in January of 1919, although it did not take effect until January 17, 1920. As a federal reservation, Prohibition of course extended to Yellowstone National Park. The nature of bootlegging activity was such that participants were not likely to keep written and photographic evidence of their endeavors, so not much about Prohibition in

Smuggler Ben F. Goe Jr. (left) was caught bootlegging in the park in 1931. Presumably this photograph was taken as a mug shot of Goe. PHOTOGRAPHER UNKNOWN, OPEN PARK NETWORK

Raymond Lynch (right) was apparently arrested at the same time as Ben Goe in the previous photograph, June 1931, presumably in the same dragnet. This must be Lynch's mug shot. PHOTOGRAPHER UNKNOWN, OPEN PARK NETWORK

the park is known with certainty. But there are a few hints about bootlegging activity in Yellowstone, still in existence a century after the fact, that if nothing else are highly entertaining.

There are, in fact, at least a few authentic photos amounting to mugshots of accused bootleggers who were arrested at Mammoth. There are other photos, apparently shot at the same time as the mugshots of the booze smugglers, of rangers pouring confiscated liquor into Clematis Creek, which is the little stream hard against the north side of the Mammoth Hot Springs Terraces. The fact that the photos even exist, shot as they were during an era (1920s) when cameras were not nearly as ubiquitous as they would later become, and especially given the fact that the shooting of the mugshots and the disposal of the confiscated liquor must have been coordinated, would seem to indicate that the whole affair was arranged for the sake of public consumption, to

Rangers pour confiscated liquor into Clematis Creek on the north side of the Mammoth Hot Springs Terraces. Given the dates on the photographs, it would seem likely that the booze being disposed of in this photograph was confiscated in the bust of the two bootleggers pictured in the two preceding photos. PHOTOGRAPHER UNKNOWN, OPEN PARK NETWORK

This barn sits behind the Old Faithful Lower Store and is still in existence today. Probably built as a carriage shed by Henry Klamer, the original owner of the Lower Store, it was used in later years by Charles A. Hamilton of Hamilton Stores to sell hay and grain to tourists traveling through the park on horseback or in horse-drawn wagons. During Prohibition, the building was rumored to have been used as a hiding place for stashes of booze that were drawn on as needed by Charles Hamilton and his cronies, especially for use on their boozy auto tours around the park. YELLOWSTONE NATIONAL PARK COLLECTION

Some old Yellowstone photos really do make it seem like they made tougher rangers in the old days. This ranger was about to head out on a horse patrol from Mammoth in the absolute dead of winter. The question is, where was he going? It would be a long, cold ride to anywhere a ranger would have to patrol. PHOTOGRAPHER UNKNOWN, OPEN PARK NETWORK

This little-known lodge was situated at Yellowstone's East Entrance, not on the actual Sylvan Pass. It was opened for business in 1924, closed for good in the mid-1930s, and torn down in 1940. It was primarily intended to be a lunch station for travelers going between Cody, Wyoming, and interior destinations within the park, but there were tents available for overnight stays. PHOTOGRAPHER UNKNOWN, OPEN PARK NETWORK

Marian Albright was the daughter of National Park Service pioneer Horace Albright and his wife, Grace. Marian was fortunate to spend many of her growing-up years at Yellowstone's headquarters at Mammoth Hot Springs, where she had the chance to interact with park wildlife on an intimate basis. She lived a long life, working as a historian, writer, and conservationist, until she passed away in 2015. PHOTOGRAPHER UNKNOWN, OPEN PARK NETWORK

Black bears have long been common near Roosevelt Lodge, as they still are today. In 1927 they were so much a part of the scene that the one in this employee group photograph on the front steps of the lodge did not attract so much as a sideways glance. JACK ELLIS HAYNES, YELLOWSTONE NATIONAL PARK COLLECTION

Superintendent Roger Toll is at left front in this photo from 1930, which was taken in front of the building at Mammoth Hot Springs known as the Pagoda for its architectural style. Others in the photograph are Horace Albright, standing just to the right of the doorway, and his daughter and probably his son standing in front of him. The unidentified man cuddling his pet mountain lion is in stark contrast to the next photograph. YELLOWSTONE NATIONAL PARK COLLECTION

Two men, probably hired as hunters or trappers by the National Park Service, pose with a dead mountain lion they killed in the park. The location of the photo was probably Mammoth. Predator control was a major goal of the park service for many decades through the late nineteenth and early twentieth centuries. From a modern management perspective, it seems counterintuitive: On the one hand the agency was eliminating predators to protect ungulates, while at the same time working to cull overpopulated herds of the latter. PHOTOGRAPHER, DATE, AND EXACT LOCATION UNKNOWN, YELLOWSTONE NATIONAL PARK COLLECTION

show that the park and its rangers were on top of things and enforcing the Volstead Act within the boundaries of the park.

On the other hand, there are shadowy stories of rangers getting together to celebrate Prohibition busts for bootlegging—and binging on confiscated alcohol in their celebrations. There is at least one such story from the Lamar Valley area, and at least one other from Lake, where Lake rangers used confiscated booze to great advantage during a party at the Lake Ranger Station after making the bust that supplied the liquor.

There is another story, this one much more substantiated, of how an old hay barn behind the Lower Hamilton Store at Old Faithful was used as a secret hideaway for large caches of liquor, beginning shortly after the enactment of Prohibition and continuing until it was finally repealed on December 5, 1933. According to sources in a position to know, and not likely to shade the details this long after the fact and after the participants passed away, Charles Hamilton of the Hamilton Store dynasty

Sylvan Pass is high in the Absaroka Mountains on the East Entrance Road, so it receives huge amounts of snowfall. In addition, the pass is prone to avalanching, with snow sliding down the steep slopes above the road and piling up to truly impressive depths. Here a rotary plow is blowing avalanched and drifted snow off the roadway, but a notation on the original photograph, taken on April 22, 1940, says that the road was closed again a short time later by yet another snow slide. PHOTOGRAPHER UNKNOWN, OPEN PARK NETWORK

Photos like this one from the mid-1930s show that crowding and traffic congestion in Yellowstone happened in the old days, too. This jam was at Riverside Geyser, which, judging by the number of onlookers gathered in the left rear of the photo, must have been about to erupt. PHOTOGRAPHER UNKNOWN, OPEN PARK NETWORK

of Yellowstone general stores periodically dispatched a lieutenant to Butte, Montana, which was known to be a central place in the region for the distribution of illegal alcohol. As the story goes, Hamilton had a large truck at his disposal, which his assistant would drive to Butte, fill with a big load of booze, and then return to Old Faithful, all in the dark in one night. Once back at Old Faithful the truck filled with "juice," in the parlance of Prohibition, would be hurriedly parked out of sight and left unloaded in the old hay barn, which originally had been built in the 1890s as a carriage shed by Henry Klamer, the original owner of the Old Faithful Lower Store (the barn still stands today, although in a dilapidated condition). Once stashed away in the hay barn, Hamilton and his cronies would draw off the load of booze as needed, often using it to fuel his famous automobile excursions around the roads of the park—on which he was often accompanied by park officials—until the load of juice was used up and it was time for Hamilton's lieutenant to make another run to Butte.

~

This touring car has driven out to the cone of Old Faithful Geyser, something completely unthinkable today. With the passengers' heads turned toward the geyser and away from the camera, it is not possible to say for sure, but the couple in the backseat may be President Warren and First Lady Florence Harding. If so, the picture would have been taken during their July 1923 visit to Yellowstone. PHOTOGRAPHER AND DATE UNKNOWN, YELLOWSTONE NATIONAL PARK COLLECTION

Another event that had major repercussions for Yellowstone during the interim years between the world wars, this one much easier to document, was the Great Depression. Again, to use annual visitation to the park as a gauge, numbers of tourists visiting Yellowstone increased steadily through the decade of the 1920s until 1929, when they totaled almost 261,000. The very next summer, which of course was the summer after the stock market crash and the onset of the Depression in October of 1929, visitation dropped to less than 228,000. From there visitation continued to diminish every year until 1934, when it not only began to recover but also resumed the inexorable long-term increase that Yellowstone has experienced since the park's inception.

Travel volume may have returned, but business in the park was so slow that many of Yellowstone's famous hotels and other properties spent much of the Great Depression, as well as most of World War II, in a shuttered condition. Because of the lack of revenue, those properties suffered from neglect due to staff and supply shortages during the 1930s and early 1940s, and so were in poor condition and far from prepared for the huge surge of visitation that followed immediately on the heels of World War

This obstruction with only one chute to allow passage was built for the purpose of counting spawning cutthroat trout running up Clear Creek from Yellowstone Lake on their annual spawn. Spawning runs on Clear Creek were astonishing in the days before the cutthroat population in the lake crashed in the late 1990s and early 2000s as a consequence of the appearance of non-native lake trout in Yellowstone Lake. The number of spawners in Clear Creek peaked at over 70,000 fish per spring in the 1970s. PHOTOGRAPHER UNKNOWN, OPEN PARK NETWORK

Here a woman is feeding a black bear outside the building that serves as the Roosevelt Lodge manager's office today, and probably did when this photo was taken in the 1930s. The woman is thought to be Isabel Haynes, and that likelihood is strengthened by the fact that Isabel's husband, Jack Ellis Haynes, took the photograph and because she was the manager of Roosevelt Lodge for a number of summers. The building behind the woman and the bear also served as the Roosevelt Lodge winterkeeper's cottage, which is likely why the window is protected with bear bars. JACK ELLIS HAYNES, YELLOWSTONE NATIONAL PARK COLLECTION

These women are not identified on the original 1930s photograph. Who were they? Where did they come from? Where did they go and what happened to them later? Whatever the answers to these and other questions, posing as they were on Grotto Geyser was probably an event they remembered and treasured for the rest of their life. PHOTOGRAPHER AND EXACT DATE UNKNOWN, OPEN PARK NETWORK

II. Most of the few maintenance workers kept on hand by park concessions during the Depression and the second war were retained in a caretaker function, clearing snow from roofs in winter, simply watching over properties in the summer, and not actively working at much upkeep of properties in their charge.

National Park Service staff likewise suffered from staff reductions during World War II, as many men were sent off to war and budget cuts severely limited the number of employees the service was able to hire and retain. The park service was only thirteen years old when the Great Depression hit and had been operating in Yellowstone without interruption for only eleven years. The Depression was followed immediately by World War II, with further suppression of manpower for the agency. Perhaps because of the smaller staff, and because of the budgetary and other hardships they faced, rangers and others employed by the park service seemed to come together during the 1930s and early 1940s, and continued to build traditions and a dedicated subculture as they and their agency matured. Perhaps the smaller staff meant that individuals had more of an opportunity to bond with each other while free of the interruptions that come with operating within a larger group, or perhaps the extra challenges they faced brought them together because of their shared devotion toward protecting the park they loved, but either way there is no question that the agency did indeed mature during these years.

CHAPTER 8

SURGE (1946–1988)

Firefighters from the California Department of Forestry, who had been brought in to help with Yellowstone's fire emergency during the summer of 1988, get out of the way as a large bull bison crosses the Grand Loop Road near the Mary Mountain trailhead in Hayden Valley. A spot fire can be seen burning at the edge of the forest at the extreme left of the frame. This day in late August

was ferociously windy, which drove this offshoot of the North Fork Fire, named the Wolf Lake Fire, across the western and central expanses of Hayden Valley before halting at the Yellowstone River. JEFF HENRY/ROCHE JAUNE PICTURES, INC.

WORLD WAR II WAS THE MOST COLOSSAL CONFLICT in the history of the world, and as such its influence reached halfway around the globe and had a profound impact on Yellowstone National Park. The war's influence on visitation was even greater than the onset of the Great Depression. After an initial drop in visitation because of the Depression, the number of visitors actually rebounded in 1934 and then set a new record each year through the summer of 1941, the last summer before the United States entered the war in December of that year. But in the summer of 1942, visitation dropped precipitously to under 200,000, down from nearly 600,000 the summer before, and then in 1943 it dropped even further to just a little over 64,000. Because of the rationing of supplies like gasoline and tires, and the other disruptions of war, the few visitors who came through the park in 1942

For many years large numbers of employees coming to work the summer season in Yellowstone arrived by train at the terminus of the Northern Pacific spur line in Gardiner, Montana, shown here in 1947. The expressions on the faces of these young people show a predictable range of emotions, from excitement to apprehension to happiness. But like most employees who worked in Yellowstone throughout the history of the park, they were in for one of the most special chapters of their lives. JACK ELLIS HAYNES, YELLOWSTONE NATIONAL PARK COLLECTION

Anna and Elizabeth Trishman were the daughters of the post carpenter at Fort Yellowstone around the turn of the twentieth century. They entered the retail business in Yellowstone in 1908, and in 1932 purchased the properties pictured here in 1947 at Canyon. The location was very close to the falls and the canyon of the Yellowstone River. Anna and Elizabeth continued to operate their retail businesses at Mammoth and Canyon until they sold to Hamilton Stores, Inc., in 1953. The structures in this photograph were removed in the early 1960s as part of the Mission 66 renovation of the Canyon area. PHOTOGRAPHER UNKNOWN, OPEN PARK NETWORK

The Old Faithful Cafeteria was situated just north of the Old Faithful Upper Store, very close to the site of the restored Haynes Photo Shop, which is now operated by Yellowstone Forever. The author remembers eating in this building in the fall of 1978, by which time it had been converted to an employee dining facility. The crowds lined up in this 1946 photograph are indicative of the unexpected rush of visitors who flooded into Yellowstone during the first summer after World War II. The park was woefully unprepared to accommodate and serve such numbers of people, especially after having seen very little visitation during the war years and the Great Depression before then. PHOTOGRAPHER UNKNOWN, OPEN PARK NETWORK

Trail rides in the Old Faithful area continued to be a popular activity well into the second half of the twentieth century. This group was staging just south of the Old Faithful Inn, near the site where Old Faithful Inn bellhops today split and stack wood for the fireplaces in the venerable building. PHOTOGRAPHER UNKNOWN, OPEN PARK NETWORK

These two children, quite likely brother and sister, were admiring the spectacle of Tower Falls on Tower Creek in the early 1950s. Then, as now, the future of Yellowstone belonged to the young and how they responded to the wonders of the park. PHOTOGRAPHER UNKNOWN, OPEN PARK NETWORK

In spite of directives against doing so, many visitors insisted on throwing objects in Morning Glory Pool and many other park thermal features. Coins thrown in, as in a wishing well, were common, as were articles of clothing that probably were thrown in based on stories of early park visitors doing their laundry in hot pots. It wasn't just coins and garments, however—the author remembers assisting with such cleanings and finding truly unexpected items in hot springs, including hand tools, pipes, and even a 1920s-era automobile tire. Nowadays it seems that attitudes have changed, and litter in hot springs is much less of a problem than it was in the not-too-distant past. PHOTOGRAPHER UNKNOWN, OPEN PARK NETWORK

These rangers in 1957 probably had been transported in this oversnow vehicle from Mammoth and were being dropped off in Hayden Valley to ski to the Mary Mountain Patrol, located near the geographic center of the park about midway between Hayden Valley on the east and the Firehole River on the west. The rangers on skis were perhaps going to the cabin to shovel its roof to prevent collapse under the late winter snow load. PHOTOGRAPHER UNKNOWN, OPEN PARK NETWORK

David Condon was a longtime interpretive ranger in Yellowstone during the mid-twentieth century. The woman standing next to the erupting columns of Clepsydra Geyser in this May 1955 photo may have been his wife. Standards were different and much more relaxed in Condon's time. In today's world, no one is allowed off the boardwalk in such close proximity to Clepsydra Geyser or any similar feature. DAVID CONDON, YELLOWSTONE NATIONAL PARK COLLECTION

and 1943 were mostly local fishermen from nearby communities and servicemen en route to distant duty reassignments. As it became more apparent that the United States and its allies were going to win the war, rationing and travel restrictions relaxed somewhat and visitation to Yellowstone increased a little, to a bit more than 85,000 in 1944 and then almost 180,000 in 1945. Almost all concessions businesses were closed during the war years, and the maintenance neglect that had begun during the Great Depression continued.

In the summer of 1946, the park experienced an unprecedented rush of visitors filled with what economists like to call pent-up demand that left them eager to head out on the road and escape the confinement brought on by four years of rationing and travel restrictions. It is an understatement to say that when 815,000 visitors surged through Yellowstone that summer, the park and its infrastructure were woefully unprepared to answer to their needs. The problems of neglected park facilities were compounded by shortages of supplies and labor in the immediate postwar

A variety of oversnow vehicles were used in the days after World War II, with some of the vehicles actually coming from the war as military surplus. This vehicle may have been a World War II–vintage Weasel, which was designed for use in the snowy reaches of Norway but not employed there because the United States and its allies never invaded that Nazi-held country. This Weasel was one of several that wound up in Yellowstone, and is shown crossing a large snowdrift that not surprisingly still forms every winter at the Golden Gate in exactly the same place as in this picture, which was shot on March 30, 1954. The canyon below Rustic Falls on Glen Creek yawns open just to the left of the Weasel. PHOTOGRAPHER UNKNOWN, OPEN PARK NETWORK

This image illustrates the large numbers of tourists that flocked to Yellowstone in the years immediately after World War II. The Fishing Bridge area has long been a favored camping area for Americans traveling to Yellowstone, as it was for Native Americans for at least 13,000 years before Yellowstone was created as a park. PHOTOGRAPHER AND EXACT DATE UNKNOWN, OPEN PARK NETWORK

period—suppliers to provide foodstuffs to feed park tourists were particularly difficult to find within the Yellowstone region.

The surge of visitors in the first summer after the war was something of an unexpected bolt out of the blue, but in another sense that summer was just the beginning of a trend that not only continued but in some respects worsened as the remaining years of the 1940s blended into the 1950s. Visitation topped 1 million for the first time in Yellowstone's history in 1948 and continued to rise, with few exceptions, every year from then on. As visitor numbers continued their relentless rise, the park's main concessioner, the Yellowstone Park Company, meanwhile was beset by financial difficulties, which compounded problems that had begun with neglected maintenance during the Great Depression and World War II. YP Company, as it was usually called, was still in debt to various

Many Yellowstone fans are surprised to learn that population control of elk and bison continued until the late 1960s. Here a helicopter was being used to drive a herd of mostly bull elk into a corral that was built near Crystal Creek, near the Lamar River bridge. The elk were probably shot and removed from the population once they were securely contained within the corral. PHOTOGRAPHER AND DATE UNKNOWN, YELLOWSTONE NATIONAL PARK COLLECTION

Another shot of elk being handled at the Crystal Creek elk catching trap. Many of the faces in this photo are familiar to the author, which points out how recently this sort of management activity still happened. It appears that these men might have been preparing to saw off this bull elk's antlers. If so, that might mean they were readying the bull for shipment elsewhere. PHOTOGRAPHER AND DATE UNKNOWN, YELLOWSTONE NATIONAL PARK COLLECTION

Another image of one of the World War II Weasels that came to Yellowstone as military surplus. This Weasel was employed to drag out the carcasses of elk shot by rangers on the Yellowstone range as a means of population reduction. The date of the photograph is probably the 1960s. YELLOWSTONE NATIONAL PARK COLLECTION

Native Americans in the region were often brought to Yellowstone during the post–World War II era to kill bison as another means of population control. They usually came to the park in late autumn or early winter, after the park had been seasonally closed to visitors but before winter snows became too deep. The men in this December 1955 photo had killed and were processing several bison along the Grand Loop Road just south of Alum Creek. JERRY BATESON, JR. COLLECTION, USED WITH PERMISSION

This ranger was one of two who made the trip to Norris from Mammoth on February 1, 1955, to clear snow from the roofs of park service buildings and to pull a snow course, which means checking the depth and water content of that year's snowpack. Apparently the ranger in this picture was not experienced with roof clearing, and also not adept at analysis of situational danger. If the snow on the roof above him had broken loose and avalanched, the ranger would have been in a very bad place indeed. PHOTOGRAPHER UNKNOWN, OPEN PARK NETWORK

The ranger on the left in this photograph appears to be the same one pictured shoveling the roof in the previous picture. Here the two men are pulling a snow course, which involves ramming a hollow pipe into the snowpack and then measuring the depth and weight of the sample thus obtained. The weight of the sample translates into a value for the water content of the snow, a factor important in forecasting hydrological phenomena such as spring runoff and summer availability of irrigation water in farmland outside Yellowstone's boundaries. PHOTOGRAPHER UNKNOWN, OPEN PARK NETWORK

railroad companies dating back to earlier years when railroads had a strong interest in Yellowstone because of the passenger traffic the park attracted. The lack of revenue during the Depression and the war had further strapped YP Company, and the upshot was that very little new construction or upkeep of park facilities was done even after the war, so shortages of lodging and other visitor services in the park continued.

~

Inadequate visitor services in national parks in general resulted in the National Park Service embarking on a major renovation program in 1956, called Mission 66, which

The Hebgen Lake earthquake of August 17, 1959, centered just a few miles outside Yellowstone's western boundary, caused great damage within the park. This photograph shows the rocky debris that fell onto the road just downhill from the Golden Gate. The landmark Pillar of Hercules is visible slightly down and to the right of center. It is obvious that travel across this causeway above the canyon of Glen Creek was not possible until after a major cleanup effort was conducted. YELLOWSTONE NATIONAL PARK COLLECTION

So severe was the 1959 earthquake that it damaged many park buildings to the point that they were deemed unsafe for occupancy. Here a tent canopy had been set up on a lawn at Mammoth to serve as a temporary office for the park superintendent. The superintendent at the time was Lem Garrison, who is pictured in the flat hat of the park service just to the left of the canopy's opening and shaking hands with the man under the sign identifying the canopy as the superintendent's office. The men lined up in front of the canopy were all important figures in the park service and concession businesses at the time. PHOTOGRAPHER AND EXACT DATE UNKNOWN, OPEN PARK NETWORK

Another casualty of the 1959 earthquake was the new Hamilton Store warehouse just inside Yellowstone's West Entrance at West Yellowstone, Montana. The cinder block walls of the structure were partially laid but not braced when the earthquake hit, so the walls came tumbling down. Hamilton Stores, Inc., and its owners were always resilient and determined, so they picked up the pieces of the fallen walls and started over. The finished building is still in service today. PHOTOGRAPHER UNKNOWN, OPEN PARK NETWORK

Jerry Bateson was a kind and quiet man who served as winterkeeper at Lake Hotel from 1950 to 1975; he worked at the same location for thirty-three summers. Winter transportation in Yellowstone for most of Jerry's tenure was by snowplane, one of which is pictured here. The conveyance was somewhat similar to an airboat in the Florida Everglades in that it was propelled by an airplane-like prop in the back, but unlike an airboat the snowplane ran across the snow on skis. In this photograph Jerry had transported a ranger to Beaverdam Creek at the south end of the Southeast Arm of Yellowstone Lake, from where the ranger embarked on a ski patrol of the Thorofare region around the Yellowstone River headwaters. During his career as a winter caretaker, Jerry Bateson suffered a serious injury to his back from the exposed propeller on the rear of his snowplane. JERRY BATESON, JR. COLLECTION, USED WITH PERMISSION

Another photograph of snowplanes in wintry Yellowstone during the 1950s. These planes came from West Yellowstone and were photographed in front of the winterkeeper's cottage behind the Old Faithful Inn. The second house in the background was also used at times to house winterkeepers. The man on the left is feeding something to the doe mule deer, which was a common practice for Old Faithful winterkeepers for many years. The winterkeeper house in the left foreground still stands behind the inn, albeit in a dilapidated condition. The second house was moved to Canyon some years ago, where it now serves as a ticket cabin for the park concession's horse corrals. LESLIE QUINN COLLECTION, USED WITH PERMISSION

These Bombardier snowcoaches were parked on the sidewalk adjacent to the East Wing of the Old Faithful Inn. They almost certainly had come in from West Yellowstone, where entrepreneurs Harold Young and Bill Nicholls had purchased two Bombardiers in 1952. The Bombardier tours into the park were the beginnings of what became a major boom in winter tourism in Yellowstone, a boom that reached its crescendo in the late 1990s and early 2000s, before the National Park Service instituted restrictions that curtailed winter visitation. LESLIE QUINN COLLECTION, USED WITH PERMISSION

These snowmobiles appear to be models from the 1960s, which was shortly after snowmobiles came into popular use. Another clue as to the date of the photograph is that the Old Faithful Snow Lodge, toward the right of the frame, appears to be closed; that building first opened for winter business during the winter of 1971–72. Early-day snowmobiles such as these were unreliable contraptions, and riders had to be skilled and prepared for mechanical breakdowns or face long walks over the snow to get back home. LESLIE QUINN COLLECTION, USED WITH PERMISSION.

was intended as an upgrade of facilities on a system-wide basis to be completed by the service's fiftieth anniversary in 1966. In Yellowstone, Mission 66 led to an entire redevelopment of the Canyon area. The beautiful Canyon Hotel, originally built in 1911, was removed and replaced with a new complex closer to Canyon Junction; most of that complex is still in existence today in the form of the lodging registration building, the building housing the gift shop, bar and restaurant, and the two retail stores presently operated by Yellowstone General Stores. The Mission 66 program also led to the construction of several hundred cabin units at Canyon, but those units were poorly built and also sited on unstable land that caused major heaving and wracking issues, so most of those cabins have now been removed and replaced with newer lodging buildings that came on line in the mid-2010s.

Mission 66 also led to the removal of the marina located in front of the Lake Yellowstone Hotel as well as the marina at Fishing Bridge. Bridge Bay Marina, two

miles south of the main Lake area, was built as a replacement and is still in service today. The Fishing Bridge RV complex with 358 RV sites was another Mission 66 project, as were employee housing upgrades at several locations around the park. Mission 66 also provided some of the initial impetus toward removing visitor facilities from West Thumb and building the Grant Village complex as a replacement, although that project was not completed until many years after the original target date of 1966.

Generally, the strategy of Mission 66 in Yellowstone was to move visitor facilities away from points of interest, as illustrated by the move from West Thumb to Grant Village, and a similar move was seriously considered to relocate services away from the Old Faithful area and build an entirely new development, to be named Firehole Village, in the Lower Geyser Basin as a

Crowds of people fishing for the Yellowstone Lake strain of cutthroat trout from the famous Fishing Bridge were common until the National Park Service banned the activity after the 1973 season. Research revealed that the area was an important spawning ground for the fish, and that fact combined with the obvious problem of angler overcrowding were good reasons for the closure. YELLOWSTONE NATIONAL PARK COLLECTION

The Trout Creek dump was located along the stream in central Hayden Valley about four miles west of the Grand Loop Road. The practice of feeding rubbish to bears for the benefit of tourists sitting on bleachers ended during World War II, but Yellowstone continued to dump refuse in open dumps around the park into the 1970s. Bears, especially the more dominant grizzlies, gathered in large numbers at such sites to feed on the trash. Here two bears are waiting for the truck to dump its load—only the snout of one can be seen at the extreme right side of the frame. YELLOWSTONE NATIONAL PARK COLLECTION

This shot may have been taken along the Grand Loop Road just north of Fishing Bridge Junction. It shows that roadside feeding of mostly black bears was technically illegal but tacitly accepted well into the 1970s. The author remembers such scenes while in Yellowstone on a family vacation in the summer of 1969. HARLAN KREDIT, YELLOWSTONE NATIONAL PARK COLLECTION

replacement. Fortunately, at least in the view of almost any Yellowstone aficionado alive today, that project never happened. In addition to the loss of the tradition and magic inherent with staying in the Old Faithful area, tangible even during the short stay typical of most visitors, a development of that size would have had an enormous impact on the mostly pristine Lower Geyser Basin, which thankfully remains the haunt of grizzly bears, bison, wolves, and other wildlife and not the location of tourist shops and noisy hotels and restaurants.

∽

The immediate postwar period in Yellowstone saw the beginnings of major shifts in attitudes toward and management of the park's famous wildlife. The spectacle of bears feeding at dumps, complete with bleacher seating for the spectating public, ended when World War II began and was not resumed when the war ended, although garbage continued to be available to bears in backcountry dumps, such as the one at

The John D. Rockefeller Parkway is the seven-mile highway that connects Yellowstone with Grand Teton National Park. A 24,000-acre corridor of land around the roadway is also protected. The people pictured were on the parkway on the day of its dedication. The 1970s park service uniforms worn by these women seem demeaning and would not likely engender respect from anyone the wearer of such a uniform might encounter. The uniforms also are in strong contrast to the park service uniform worn by the man behind them. YELLOWSTONE NATIONAL PARK COLLECTION

An unknown park ranger tests the water of Great Fountain Geyser in 1977. Presumably she found that it was hot. JEREMY SCHMIDT, YELLOWSTONE NATIONAL PARK COLLECTION

Rabbit Creek near Old Faithful and another along Trout Creek in Hayden Valley, until the early 1970s. Roadside feeding of bears by tourists, although technically illegal, was tacitly allowed until the early 1970s, when prohibitions against the practice started to be more strictly enforced. The rather abrupt closing of the backcountry dumps as a source of food for bears, along with the elimination of food they had grown accustomed to scrounging along roads and in developed areas, led to a large number of bears becoming problem animals and consequently being killed in management removals. As a result, bear populations declined quite sharply in the 1970s, with as few as an estimated 136 grizzly bears left in the Greater Yellowstone Ecosystem by 1975, the year the Interagency Grizzly Bear Study Team (a consortium of involved government agencies) was formed to study and monitor the animals. Even before the formation of the IGBST, the famous brothers John and Frank Craighead had begun their landmark study of grizzly bears in Yellowstone in 1959. The Craigheads were pioneers in their field, and their work has influenced wildlife research ever since their Yellowstone project ended in 1971, when a dispute between the brothers and the National Park Service over bear management philosophy led to a termination of their research access to the park.

In a measure to save the bison from extirpation in Yellowstone, a captive herd had been bred and fed at the park's Buffalo Ranch in Lamar Valley since 1907, but supplemental feeding of hay grown on cultivated and irrigated flats along the Lamar River ended in 1946. In another vestige of earlier times, live shipments of both bison and elk to reduce herd sizes continued until the late 1960s. Other herd reductions in the form of capture and slaughter, as well as direct shooting of the animals in the field by park rangers, continued until 1967. Cessation of bison ranching and the killing of both bison and elk was part of an overall move by the National Park Service toward a more hands-off approach toward park management, reflecting a growing desire to allow natural processes to occur as much as possible.

The same push to restore a more natural Yellowstone was also behind major changes in the approach to the park's fisheries and the sport of fishing. Many of Yellowstone's waters were barren of fish when the park was created, but stocking programs began as early as 1890. Non-native fish, including brown, rainbow, brook, and lake trout, were stocked in many park lakes and streams until as late as 1933. Some stocking of non-natives took place in waters in which fish were absent, while other plants were made in waters already occupied by native fish. In almost all cases, the introduced non-native fish were extremely injurious to native species, either preying directly on them or out-competing them for habitat. Stocking programs were instituted for native fish, too, with spawning fish trapped from natural spawning grounds and stripped of eggs and milt

Dave Mattson of the Interagency Grizzly Bear Study Team records data from a winterkilled cow elk on an island in the Little Firehole River in Biscuit Basin in late winter of 1986. Dave did cutting-edge research on Yellowstone's grizzly bears from the 1970s through the 1990s. This winterkill project, in which he partnered with this author, revealed many fascinating details about ungulate use of the geyser basins as winter range, as well as a great deal of information about how grizzly bears used the bonanza of carrion they found in those basins when they emerged from their winter dens. One of the striking correlations discovered was that the average peak of winterkill for both elk and bison was March 25, and during the eight-year period during which the study was conducted, the first grizzly bear tracks of the spring were always found in the geyser basins within one day of that date. JEFF HENRY/ROCHE JAUNE PICTURES, INC.

National Park Service bear manager Sandi Fowler uses a telemetry device in an attempt to locate radio-collared Bear #83 near Beach Springs in late autumn of 1986. Sandi worked for the National Park Service for many years in the 1970s and 1980s. The bear she was searching for was a problem bear accustomed to human foods, and in spite of great efforts to rehabilitate her, she had to be removed from the Yellowstone population in a management action the following year. PHOTO BY JEFF HENRY/ROCHE JAUNE PICTURES, INC.

Ranger Dave Spirtes tries to save Bear #38's life by giving her mouth-to-mouth breathing. The radio-collared bear had been tranquilized prior to being moved by helicopter in the late summer of 1985, and unfortunately collapsed onto the transmitter of her radio collar and suffocated. Rangers Gary Brown and Colette Daigle-Berg are also in the frame, as are Les Herman and an unidentified female member of Yellowstone National Park's helitack crew. JEFF HENRY/ROCHE JAUNE PICTURES, INC.

that were used in hatchery settings to propagate more offspring than, it was thought, natural spawning would produce. The thrust of all this was, of course, to create more sport fishing opportunities for park visitors, which in turn was part of an overall push by park proponents to turn Yellowstone into a desirable venue for recreation and thereby develop a constituency to ensure the long-term survival of the national park experiment. But attitudes changed, and artificial propagation and stocking even of native species were phased out in the late 1950s. In a similar vein, more restrictive regulations on size and bag limits were instituted as philosophies trended away from profligacy and toward nonconsumptive catch-and-release sport fishing.

≈

Visitation to Yellowstone continued to grow, topping the 2 million mark for the first time in 1965 and rapidly soaring beyond that mark in subsequent years, while during the same time period ideologies evolved away from seeing Yellowstone as a playground and more toward viewing it as a fragile ecological treasure worthy of even greater levels of protection. With the growing interest in the ecology of Yellowstone, more and more research projects came on line as the postwar years progressed, academic research aimed at finding out more about Yellowstone and how its natural processes worked.

An episode illustrating how increasing knowledge of the park's natural systems led to management actions that in turn led to conflict between competing interests was the Fishing Bridge controversy that began in the 1960s. Research revealed that the Fishing Bridge area was not only prime habitat for grizzly bears but also astride an important travel corridor for the animals. This should not have been a surprise, because Fishing Bridge is located at a key geographic site at the outlet of

Yellowstone Lake, and as such it is at an intersection of travel routes leading around the shores of Yellowstone Lake and up and down the Yellowstone River. The area also includes a mix of productive habitats in close proximity. These elements were the reason the area was not only attractive to bears and other species of wildlife, but also to indigenous peoples who had lived at the site for thousands of years before Yellowstone was created as a park. The same elements also influenced the development of Fishing Bridge at the site just a few years after the park was designated—the environmental and geographic qualities of the area held appeal for modern humans, too, just as they did for prehistoric humans and wildlife.

Meanwhile, the development on the west side of Yellowstone Lake, named Grant Village, had first been proposed in the 1950s as part of the park service's Mission 66 program, but after some initial work, its construction had languished for years. To make a long and complicated story short, removal of the developments at Fishing Bridge became a cause célèbre for environmental groups in the 1970s as a measure to save the Yellowstone grizzly bear, which by that time faced the very real possibility of extirpation from the ecosystem. The strategy was to replace facilities removed from Fishing Bridge with new developments at Grant Village, which was all well and good until still further research revealed that the Grant area was prime grizzly bear habitat, too, in the form of several cutthroat trout spawning streams that flowed through the area on their way to Yellowstone Lake. Legal and emotional conflicts ensued and continued for years between factions generally characterized as commercial interests versus environmentalists, with the resolution being the removal of much of the development at Fishing Bridge and the construction of new lodging buildings and other services at Grant Village. The upshot was that while some saw the trade-off as a reasonable compromise, others saw the result as neither here nor there—that too much of the commercial development remained near grizzly bear habitat at Fishing Bridge, while a great deal of new development intruded into another area of important bear habitat at Grant Village. On the other hand, commercial concerns, especially those located east of the park and close to Fishing Bridge, felt their interests had been compromised by the loss of so much development near the Yellowstone Lake outlet, especially the removal of 308 sites in the government campground and hundreds of tourist cabins that had been located behind the still existing Fishing Bridge General Store.

In spite of residual dissatisfaction with the decisions regarding the Fishing Bridge/Grant Village controversy, tensions over the matter naturally dissipated as the years of the 1980s passed. But the issue was still simmering when the great Yellowstone fires of 1988 flared and became the new focus of attention. The fires, in turn, became controversial; many critics believed they were the result of an unrealistic park policy that

Ken Hansen and an unidentified firefighter spray water onto the roof of the historic Old Faithful Inn on September 7, 1988, the day the great North Fork Fire stormed through the Old Faithful complex. The ferocious winds that day are evident from the taut flag on top of the inn, while a few seemingly unconcerned tourists walk past the firefighters on their way to the south door of the inn. Curiously, Yellowstone was still open to visitors, even on this smoke-shrouded day of extreme fire danger. JEFF HENRY/ROCHE JAUNE PICTURES, INC.

Firefighter Amy Recker of Yellowstone National Park poses with a foaming hose in Hayden Valley on August 25, 1988. Amy was laying a bed of foam, some of which can be seen on the ground behind her, all around a disabled fire truck that had broken down in front of the advancing Wolf Lake Fire. Amy's efforts were successful—the disabled fire truck lived to fight another day, as did Amy. JEFF HENRY/ROCHE JAUNE PICTURES, INC.

allowed fires to burn until they exploded out of control. The reality was different—as a phenomenon resulting from a combination of extreme drought, heat, and wind, the Yellowstone fires were an unstoppable force of nature, no more controllable than a hurricane or an earthquake. (The story of the historic Yellowstone fires of 1988 is addressed in more detail in Chapter 9.)

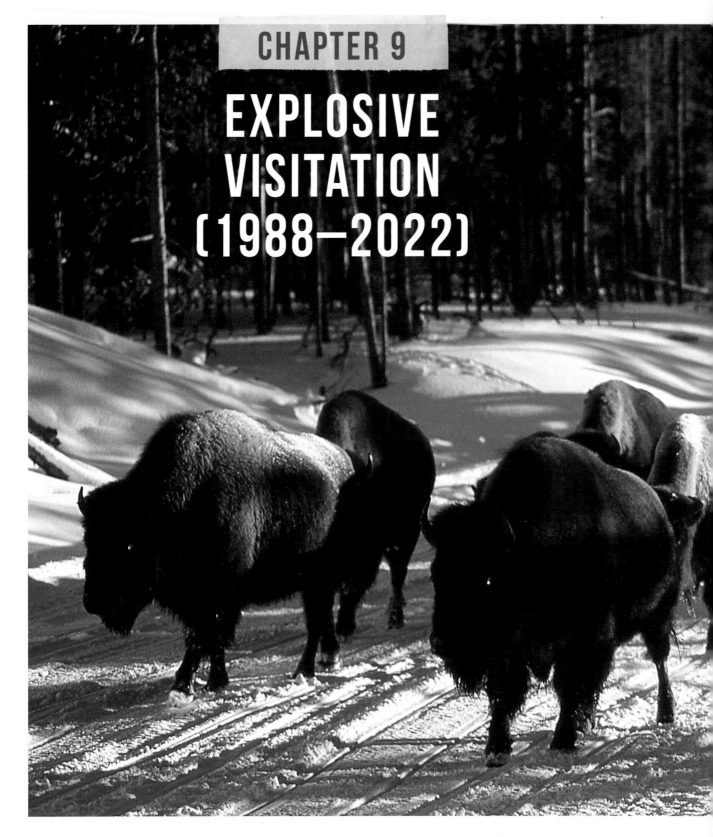

CHAPTER 9

EXPLOSIVE VISITATION (1988–2022)

Snowy road surfaces packed and groomed for the benefit of snowmobiles and snowcoaches also provide easy migration corridors for several species of Yellowstone's wildlife. The drawback, from the standpoint of the animals, is that while traveling on the groomed roads they are often subjected to the stress of passing traffic. And it's not just snowmobiles—a close look in the shadows at the

far end of the visible road in this photograph shows a snowcoach also waiting its turn to pass this herd of bison near the mouth of Mallard Creek on the Grand Loop Road. This picture was taken in the 1990s, and because of management decisions that have since reduced winter traffic, conflicts between wildlife and snow vehicles have lessened. JEFF HENRY/ROCHE JAUNE PICTURES, INC.

THE 1988 FIRES IN YELLOWSTONE BEGAN IN JUNE, when lightning strikes ignited blazes in several different locations in the park's backcountry. The fires that started at that time smoldered for a few weeks, with the Fan Fire in the northwestern corner of the park being the first to draw substantial attention when it flared up on July 1. After that date fire activity picked up, as dry and abnormally hot and windy weather continued through July. By the end of the month, most of the major fires that ultimately would burn more than 800,000 acres of Yellowstone National Park (over 1.3 million acres in the ecosystem) had started and were at least in their beginning stages.

The elements contributing to the great fires extended back at least to the winter of 1986–87, which was dry to a record- or nearly record-breaking extent. The summer of 1987 was abnormally wet, but the winter of 1987–88

Masses of snowmobiles enter Yellowstone's West Entrance on February 18, 1995. By the mid-1990s the popularity of snowmobiling in Yellowstone had exploded. There were problems with congestion, especially at key points at certain times of day, and pollution—snow machines in those days were the grossly polluting two-stroke variety that not only belched toxic exhaust but also were so inefficient, that they expelled some of their fuel in an unburned state directly onto the snow. This photograph was taken on President's Day weekend, which historically was one of the heaviest traffic days of the winter season. JEFF HENRY/ROCHE JAUNE PICTURES, INC.

It's not just the oversnow roads that offer more easily negotiated travel routes for Yellowstone's wildlife. In this photo taken near Geode Creek on the Mammoth-Tower Road, a large group of bison are traveling toward Mammoth. Bison, especially, are an issue on machine-packed or plowed roadways. They follow such routes in a natural tendency to move to lower elevations during winter weather. The trouble for the animals is that such migration to lower elevations takes them outside the boundaries of Yellowstone National Park, mostly into the state of Montana, where they are seen as a nuisance, and many are shot by hunters recruited by the state or shipped to slaughterhouses. JEFF HENRY/ROCHE JAUNE PICTURES, INC.

The National Park Service has built holding corrals near its northern boundary in the area of Stephens Creek, just west of Yellowstone's North Entrance. Many bison are herded into the corrals as they try to migrate to lower elevations in Montana, and from those corrals most are then loaded onto trucks and shipped to slaughter. In this photo from the early 2000s, members of a herd of captured bison are awaiting their fate. JEFF HENRY/ROCHE JAUNE PICTURES, INC.

was another dry one, although not as dry as the previous winter. The spring of 1988 was abnormally cool and wet, which turned out to be a curse in disguise; the plentiful moisture that spring served to grow a profuse crop of forbs and grasses, which in turn became fine tinder for the fires that sprang to life later that season. The immediate cause of the fires was the unprecedentedly hot, dry, and windy weather that Yellowstone experienced beginning in May 1988. A longer-term cause leading to the great conflagrations of 1988 was that the fire-evolved forests of the area had not burned to any considerable extent for many decades, which led to a massive buildup of fuels stored in mature, even moribund, forests in an environment where vegetation tends to grow and accumulate faster than it dies and decays.

Not all the Yellowstone fires in 1988 were caused by lightning. In fact, the largest, the North Fork Fire, which burned well over 400,000 acres, started in Idaho's

After capture at Stephens Creek, bison are moved from one paddock to another via a series of chutes, such as the one pictured here. In the chutes biological samples are taken from the animals, and the chutes also serve as corridors to trucks waiting to load and haul them to slaughter.
JIM PEACO, YELLOWSTONE NATIONAL PARK COLLECTION

Many bison that avoid capture and confinement in the park service corrals and make it across the park boundary are shot by hunters. This photograph was taken a short distance outside Gardiner, Montana, and shows a large bull bison and the hunters who are processing his carcass, along with park ranger Rick McAdam and Montana state game warden Hank Fabich. Electric Peak is the snowy mountain in the background, while Sepulcher Mountain is closer and to the left of Electric. JIM PEACO, YELLOW-STONE NATIONAL PARK COLLECTION

Val Asher and Alice Whitelaw carry a trapped and tranquilized wolf out of the Canadian bush near Hinton, Alberta. Val and Alice played a large role in capturing the first fourteen wolves that were taken from Alberta and brought to Yellowstone in the first wave of wolf reintroductions into the park in January 1995. The restoration of wolves to Yellowstone was a major event in the history of the park.
JEFF HENRY/ROCHE JAUNE PICTURES, INC.

Targhee National Forest west of the park when a woodcutter carelessly discarded a cigarette. The Huck Fire, just south of Yellowstone, was started when a tree blew into a high-powered electrical line near the Flagg Ranch resort on August 20, the day known forever after as Black Saturday. Still another of the major fires, the Hellroaring Fire, started north of the park when an outfitter was not sufficiently mindful of sparks flying from his camp stove. All the human-caused fires were fought from their outset, as were all fires of any origin, both inside and outside the park, after July 15.

The national media largely missed the Yellowstone fire story in its earlier stages, and when they finally caught on to the magnitude of the situation later in the summer, they often got the story wrong by sensationally stating that the blazes would ruin Yellowstone forever. They also were often mistaken when they claimed that park managers had allowed the situation to develop with what they erroneously described as a "let burn policy," as opposed to the more accurate description of "prescribed fire" preferred by the park service, with the latter term referring to the benefits derived from allowing naturally caused fires to progress through fire-dependent ecosystems in areas away from human development.

The post-fire era in Yellowstone began in the spring of 1989 with a plethora of media returning to Yellowstone to capture the fire recovery story in what often seemed to be something of a do-over or an attempt to make up for the fact that the same media had

The entire first contingent of fourteen Canadian wolves that were brought to Yellowstone in January 1995. In this photo they have been tranquilized and laid out on a garage floor near Hinton, Alberta, in preparation for to being loaded on a plane and flown to the United States. JEFF HENRY/ROCHE JAUNE PICTURES, INC.

After arriving in Yellowstone the Canadian wolves were released into holding pens, where they were kept and supplementally fed while they acclimated to their new surroundings. Individuals who released the animals from their individual shipping crates were usually high-status officials, most of whom had been involved in the program to bring wolves back to Yellowstone. This shot was taken at a holding pen on Blacktail Plateau. JEFF HENRY/ROCHE JAUNE PICTURES, INC.

Rick McIntyre began working with Yellowstone's wolves almost immediately on their release from the holding pens in the spring of 1995. He continued the work almost every day for many years, splitting his time between observation and research on the animals and providing information about wolves to the visiting public. Rick has retired from the National Park Service now, but he still ventures into Lamar Valley early almost every morning before returning to his home to work on a series of books to document the restoration of wolves to Yellowstone. JEFF HENRY/ROCHE JAUNE PICTURES, INC.

Doug of the Yellowstone Wolf Project in the field with assistants and the wolves he has darted with a tranquilizer during a helicopter capture operation. Doug Smith has devoted his entire career to wildlife research, specializing in wolves, and has managed the Yellowstone Wolf Project since its inception. As an excellent public speaker and presenter, Doug has also developed a passionate following among Yellowstone wolf admirers. DOUG SMITH, USED WITH PERMISSION

Interpretive ranger Wayne Wolfersberger gives an early morning presentation in Hayden Valley. The sun was just above the eastern horizon and mist was rising off the Yellowstone River when Wayne met the visiting public at Grizzly Overlook. Wayne was stationed at the Fishing Bridge Visitor Center, so he had made the drive from there to Hayden Valley before he began his work interacting with park visitors. JEFF HENRY/ROCHE JAUNE PICTURES, INC.

The Yellowstone fires of 1988 became such a big story that the president of the United States was moved to visit the park the following spring to see the aftermath for himself. Here Yellowstone's chief of research, John Varley, apparently is explaining fire ecology to President George H. W. Bush at a site along Fountain Flats Drive not far from Ojo Caliente Spring. JIM PEACO, YELLOWSTONE NATIONAL PARK COLLECTION

In another presidential visit, National Park Service interpretive specialist Katy Duffy explains the workings of the features of the Upper Geyser Basin to President Barack Obama. The forty-fourth president of the United States brought his entire family to visit Yellowstone in August 2009. Katy was greatly honored to meet President Obama and cannot speak highly enough of him. JIM PEACO, YELLOWSTONE NATIONAL PARK COLLECTION

An assistant hands the next artillery round to Wes Miles while Brad Ross waits to load the 75mm recoilless rifle and fire the next shot. The recoilless model pictured here in a February 29, 1996, photograph has since been replaced by a larger-caliber cannon. The purpose of the artillery is, of course, to control avalanche danger on Yellowstone's Sylvan Pass. JEFF HENRY/ROCHE JAUNE PICTURES, INC.

A female mountain bluebird carries nesting material into a cavity in a subalpine fir scorched by Yellowstone's 1988 fires, five years after the burn in 1993. The National Park Service went to great lengths to promote the idea of 1988's great fires as a natural occurrence with significant ecological benefits. This photograph, taken near Yellowstone's Biscuit Basin, would seem to lend credence to that point of view. JEFF HENRY/ROCHE JAUNE PICTURES, INC.

Interest in the Yellowstone fires and their aftermath spawned a great deal of research in the years following 1988. Here botanist Don DeSpain points out a detail to assistants including Pat Terletsky, the woman in the red jacket. The site was near the junction of the Chittenden Road to Mount Washburn with the Grand Loop Road, an area that burned particularly hot when the North Fork Fire stormed through in September 1988. JEFF HENRY/ROCHE JAUNE PICTURES, INC.

Regeneration of lodgepole pine seedlings was profuse after the 1988 fires, beginning in the spring of 1989. Here seedlings are growing up between the fallen logs of trees killed in the North Fork Fire near Harlequin Lake, just west of Madison Junction. JEFF HENRY/ROCHE JAUNE PICTURES, INC.

Ranger Mark Marschall with his horse outside the Fern Lake patrol cabin north of Pelican Valley. Mark had a long history of working in Yellowstone, starting as a gas pumper for the company furnishing fuel to the traveling public, and extending through more than twenty years with the National Park Service. It is probably safe to say, however, that his favorite assignments during all that time involved working in Yellowstone's backcountry, as he was doing here in the late autumn of 1996. JEFF HENRY/ROCHE JAUNE PICTURES, INC.

This photograph was taken at the Norris Soldier Station on August 25, 1991, which was the seventy-fifth anniversary of the National Park Service. Park service employees attending the celebration and dressed in period garb in this picture include: front row, left to right: Rich Jehle, Laura Long, Dave Price, and Roger Andrasick; back row, left to right: unknown in striped shirt, Rick McAdam, John Whitman, and Tom Tankersley. JEFF HENRY/ROCHE JAUNE PICTURES, INC.

The year 2016 brought not only the 100th anniversary of the National Park Service, but also the 125th of the Lake Yellowstone Hotel. Longtime Lake-area employees and couple Dale Fowler and Crystal Cassidy were all dressed up for the occasion. JEFF HENRY/ROCHE JAUNE PICTURES, INC.

Interpretive ranger John Rhoades explains the workings of Grand Geyser to a throng of listeners on the boardwalk in the Upper Geyser Basin. Interpretive rangers are devoted to their jobs and consequently are knowledgeable and eager to educate the traveling public about the wonders of Yellowstone. They perform an extremely important function in helping visitors appreciate the park, which in turn goes a long way toward developing and maintaining a constituency to support Yellowstone and similar reserves. JEFF HENRY/ROCHE JAUNE PICTURES, INC.

largely missed the mark with their reports on the happenings of the previous summer. The increased level of media attention that came to the park late in the fire season of 1988 and the spring of 1989 never fully receded, and Yellowstone as a seasonal backwater was never quite so quiet again. Yellowstone's higher profile on the national stage would have major ramifications for the park as the years after 1989 progressed.

~

Wolves were eliminated from Yellowstone during predator programs of the late nineteenth and early twentieth centuries. The species probably ceased to be viable in the park in 1926 when two pups were taken from a den near Soda Butte Creek. The pups were hauled to park headquarters in Mammoth, where they were posed for photographs with bureaucrats before being killed by park rangers. After that incident

Ranger John Lounsbury, the district ranger at Lake at the time, was traveling on a snowmobile to Mammoth for a meeting at park headquarters when this photograph was taken in Hayden Valley, with the temperature at minus 30 degrees Fahrenheit. JEFF HENRY/ROCHE JAUNE PICTURES, INC.

Famed undersea explorer Bob Ballard, seen standing on the boardwalk with his hand on his thigh in this photograph, came to Yellowstone to film in the spring of 1997. Castle Geyser can be seen steaming behind Ballard, and among other feats on this visit, Ballard plumbed a camera into the depths of scalding Crested Pool, a short distance away from Castle Geyser. JEFF HENRY/ROCHE JAUNE PICTURES, INC.

there were scattered sightings of the big canines that possibly were legitimate, but it is almost certain that there was no sustainable reproduction of the species. The absence of wolves in Yellowstone during the decades that followed caused a wide range of ripple effects on the ecosystem. Some of the effects were obvious, such as elk populations that boomed in the absence of predation. Other effects were more subtle, such as the decline in numbers of bird species that relied on riparian brush for habitat but found such habitat scarce because of overbrowsing by those same throngs of elk.

The first articulations suggesting that it was feasible and a good idea to restore wolves to Yellowstone began not long after the species had been eliminated in the park in the 1920s. As soon as the early 1940s, the famous biologists Adolph Murie and Aldo Leopold pointed out that there was enough space in the Yellowstone ecosystem for viable populations of wolves to exist without unduly competing with commercial pursuits outside the park and in the less stringently protected preserves that surrounded it. From that time on, more and more voices were added to what became

Interpretive ranger Roy Wood escorts a group of schoolchildren through a burned forest near Frog Rock on Blacktail Plateau in September 1991, almost exactly three years after the monstrous North Fork Fire roared through the area. The schoolchildren were fascinated by what Roy had to tell them. JEFF HENRY/ROCHE JAUNE PICTURES, INC.

Interpretive ranger Arden Bailey gestures to drive home a point about the Upper Geyser Basin to a family of visitors. Bailey was roving the geyser basin on a bike at the time this picture was taken on July 13, 1998. He has worked at a variety of jobs in Yellowstone for well over forty years and is one of the most knowledgeable people alive on subjects concerning Yellowstone's geology. JEFF HENRY/ROCHE JAUNE PICTURES, INC.

Wildlife researcher Tiffany Potter and tracking specialist James Halfpenny measure some old, snowed-in lynx tracks near LeHardy's Rapids in 2002. Lynx are present in Yellowstone, but apparently only in very low numbers. JEFF HENRY/ROCHE JAUNE PICTURES, INC.

The National Park Service changed winter regulations in Yellowstone before the start of the 2003–04 season. The new changes included a ban on unsupervised snowmobile tours through the park, as well as a mandate that all snowmobiles used in the park be four-stroke machines to reduce noise and pollution. Regulations have since been amended to allow some unguided, private snowmobile parties to tour through the park on an independent basis, but such parties still have to use machines employing the best available technology. This photograph was taken on the park's West Entrance Road and shows a permitted guide leading a group tour into the park. JEFF HENRY/ROCHE JAUNE PICTURES, INC.

The restoration of wolves to Yellowstone lent a whole new dimension to the ecological scene. It is always thrilling to find their huge tracks in the mud or snow. The author's left hand is included in this photograph to give a sense of scale. JEFF HENRY/ROCHE JAUNE PICTURES, INC.

an environmental clamoring to restore wolves to Yellowstone, and the restoration was begun in January 1995 when fourteen wolves that had been captured in Alberta were transported to the park. There was considerable local and regional opposition to the plan to restore wolves to Yellowstone, to the point where the fourteen transplants arrived in the park guarded by an armed convoy.

Once in the park, the newly arrived wolves were split into groups, each of which was held in a separate acclimation pen for a little over two months before being released to range across Yellowstone. The first round of pioneering wolves

was joined by a second group of seventeen transplants, also from Canada, that were brought to the park early in 1996. The wolves did remarkably well in Yellowstone, having plenty of space and large herds of ungulates that had at most only an ancestral memory of the danger posed by wolf packs. By the mid-2000s wolf populations within Yellowstone National Park topped out at more than 170 animals, although those numbers then declined a bit as the population adjusted based on the available habitat and fewer ungulates, whose numbers declined because of the increased levels of predation and other factors, such as ongoing drought in Yellowstone. Exotic diseases like distemper and mange, which probably originated with domestic dogs, also took a toll. Distemper has been an especially deadly factor, with five separate outbreaks of the disease occurring in Yellowstone wolves over the last twenty years. Yellowstone wolves have become tremendously popular with the public, so much so that some of their fans have created social media sites devoted to the animals. Indeed, wolves have become so popular that park researchers and managers who work with them, like Rick McIntyre and Doug Smith, have achieved celebrity status among wildlife aficionados.

~

Winter visitation to Yellowstone continued to surge through 1988 and all through the years of controversy leading up to and continuing beyond the reintroduction of wolves to the park in 1995 and 1996. Growth was so unexpectedly rapid that more and more visitor facilities were overwhelmed as the winter seasons progressed. The Old Faithful Snow Lodge, for example, was

This photograph dates to the days when snowmobiles were more or less unrestricted in the park. Two of the primary complaints against snowmobiles at that time were that they were noisy and polluting. This National Park Service employee was managing equipment and collecting data on both factors at the West Entrance.
JEFF HENRY/ROCHE JAUNE PICTURES, INC.

After a long period of quiescence, Steamboat Geyser in the Norris Geyser Basin erupted in March 2018. Atmospheric conditions at the time of the eruption must have been just right for water ejected from the tallest geyser in the world to form a lovely tapestry of icicles on the surrounding trees after the hot water cooled and fell back to earth. Here, the author's daughter, Mariah Gale Henry, gets up close and personal to photograph the wonder of it all. JEFF HENRY/ROCHE JAUNE PICTURES, INC.

Bear management specialist Kerry Gunther records data on a winterkilled cow bison carcass in Fairy Meadow in the Lower Geyser Basin. Beginning in the 1970s, Kerry has worked almost his entire career at bear management in Yellowstone. In this 1991 photo he was conducting a monitoring survey as a continuation of a more in-depth study begun several years earlier by the author and the Interagency Grizzly Bear Study Team. JEFF HENRY/ROCHE JAUNE PICTURES, INC.

Non-native lake trout were first discovered in Yellowstone Lake by a fishing guide named Johnny Blair in 1993, and then they were officially identified by biologists the following year. This picture was taken just two years after that, in late July 1996, and shows a layout of lake trout removed from the lake by a gill netting operation. Fittingly, one of the lake trout has a much smaller native cutthroat trout in its mouth in what amounted to a death grip for both fish. It is remarkable that the non-native lakers reproduced and grew so quickly that there were this many of this size just three years after the first hint they had been illegally introduced into Yellowstone Lake. The appearance of lake trout in the big lake was and continues to be an ecological catastrophe. JEFF HENRY/ROCHE JAUNE PICTURES, INC.

Rangers Jeremiah Smith (by the snowmobile) and Wes Miles (with the shovel in his hand) work to retrieve a snowmobile that Miles had earlier driven over a steep embankment during a whiteout at Grizzly Overlook in Hayden Valley. The National Park Service maintenance supervisor at Canyon, Shelby Coy, looks on as the operation moves toward using a heavy piece of equipment to drag the snowmobile back to the road. Fortunately, neither Wes Miles nor the snow machine were seriously harmed in the accident. JEFF HENRY/ROCHE JAUNE PICTURES, INC.

originally built as a registration building for the many tourist cabins that sat behind the building at the time of its construction. The building was poorly designed for winter operation—it suffered with roofs leaking from snowmelt and ice dams—and was generally too small to house and feed the number of tourists who were demanding more and more of such services as the 1980s and 1990s passed by. Fuel storage capacity in the park was challenged, too, as the numbers of both snowcoaches and snowmobiles increased. As it was impossible to resupply subterranean fuel tanks in the park when roads were covered with several feet of snow, it became necessary for concessioner Yellowstone Park Service Stations to redirect traffic to first one set of its fuel stations and then another as a way of keeping up with demand. There was also the risk that overpumping buried fuel tanks could lend buoyancy to the emptied tanks, leading to the danger that they might actually pop out of the ground.

Winter visitation to Yellowstone, especially on snowmobiles, became a large source of contention between environmental and commercial concerns, which only increased as the 1990s blended into the 2000s. Matters came to a head in the winter of 2003–04, when the park service decreed that private snowmobiles would no longer be allowed into Yellowstone, and instead, snowmobilers could enter only as part of a for-

Ranger Julie Hannaford writes a ticket to an illegal fisherman in Hayden Valley. Fishing was banned on the Yellowstone River many years ago in favor of the valley's wildlife and the viewing opportunities they offered to visitors passing through the beautiful valley. Mount Washburn is in the background of this picture. JEFF HENRY/ROCHE JAUNE PICTURES, INC.

mal tour conducted by a licensed guide. Concomitant with this directive was another that banned noisy two-cycle snow machines, replacing those more polluting machines with quieter, more energy efficient four-cycle models that spewed less toxic exhaust. Quotas were also instituted to limit the number of snowmobiles entering the park. Those limitations had a particular impact on visitation during key winter holidays.

These regulatory measures were, needless to say, highly controversial. Commercial interests, especially in gateway communities around the park, were upset because they

Two wildlife researchers set up a deadfall trap for live capture of wolverines near Sylvan Lake along Yellowstone's East Entrance Road. Wolverine tracks are occasionally found in Yellowstone, but sightings of the animals are much more rare. Probably never abundant even in pre-Columbian times, these largest members of the mustelid family generally have fared poorly because of habitat destruction and fragmentation, and even reserves like Yellowstone are probably not sufficiently large to support a self-sustaining population. JEFF HENRY/ROCHE JAUNE PICTURES, INC.

The Olympic flame was carried by runners through Yellowstone in 2002. Here the flame has been passed from a torch carried by hand to a basin of fire on the boardwalk by Old Faithful Geyser. Various park dignitaries then addressed a large crowd of onlookers who had gathered for the event in spite of a heavy snowstorm. JEFF HENRY/ROCHE JAUNE PICTURES, INC.

Rangers Patti Bean and George Sechrist work to build a quinzhee in front of the Canyon Visitor Center. A quinzhee is similar to an igloo in that it is a dome-shaped structure built of snow for shelter in extreme winter conditions. The difference is that a quinzhee, rather than being built out of sawn blocks of snow like an igloo, is first made by piling up a mound of snow and then excavating an opening and hollowing out a cavity in its interior. This photograph was taken in February 1996 during a winter with very heavy snowfall. JEFF HENRY/ROCHE JAUNE PICTURES, INC.

Old Faithful Snow Lodge employees Rebekah Houck and Robert Shirer were out grooming cross-country ski trails when this photograph was taken behind the Old Faithful Lodge on a snowy day in December 2014. As is the case for most park employees, they were having the time of their lives. JEFF HENRY/ROCHE JAUNE PICTURES, INC.

National Park Service interpretive ranger John Rhoades helps a visitor from France understand the map of the Upper Geyser Basin. The photograph was taken near Castle Geyser on July 13, 1998. JEFF HENRY/ROCHE JAUNE PICTURES, INC.

saw their business opportunities diminish and because they were forced to keep more employees on the payroll to provide the guides who were required to accompany tours into the park. The requirement to use four-stroke snowmobiles also led to complaints, as such machines tend to be more expensive, and that, coupled with the fact that the park set limits on the numbers of snow machines entering the park on a daily basis, meant rentals might be difficult to obtain.

Many individuals disliked the new regulations because of the ban on solo outings. People interested in, say, bird-watching in Yellowstone's interior were no longer able to pursue their interests by traveling to a likely spot and then waiting for a hoped-for species to show up. Photographers likewise could not expect other members of a guided tour to also wait for the light to change or for an unusual wildlife behavior to take place in front of their lens. People questioned why it was permissible for a wildlife watcher to drive alone to Lamar Valley (plowed in winter) on Yellowstone's Northern Range and spend the day watching wolves, while a person desiring to engage in a similar activity in the more wintry expanses of Yellowstone's interior could not engage in

This photograph shows the former Old Faithful Snow Lodge with the new Snow Lodge under construction at the left rear of the frame. The old Snow Lodge was originally built as a registration building for summer use for the many tourist cabins situated behind it; it was then used for winter concessions operations beginning with the winter of 1971–72. Construction on the new Snow Lodge began in the summer of 1997, progressed through the following winter, and then led to the removal of the old building in the spring of 1998. After the old structure had been removed, the new Snow Lodge was then extended onto the site of the former; it first opened for winter business in December 1998. JEFF HENRY/ROCHE JAUNE PICTURES, INC.

This is a photograph of the new Old Faithful Snow Lodge on the day it first opened for a winter season, on December 21, 1998. As fate would have it, and perhaps appropriately, the temperature was 45 degrees below zero on the building's first day of winter operation. The first snowcoach driver to pull up to the front of the building that morning was Jim Berry, a longtime driver out of West Yellowstone, Montana. JEFF HENRY/ROCHE JAUNE PICTURES, INC.

the same sort of activity by making a similarly individualized trip on a snowmobile. Another frequent complaint, and one that indeed had substance, was that under the new guidelines winter trips into Yellowstone were expensive, to the point that many felt the common person had been priced out of the market.

As a partial response to these concerns, the park service initiated a program a few years after the winter of 2003–04 in which individuals or small groups could apply for a limited number of unguided permits to travel through the park on specific dates without a guide. The machines used on such tours had to comply with noise and pollution standards set by the park service, and of course had to be the four-cycle variety of snowmobile. Individuals fortunate enough to be drawn in the lottery for the unguided trips also had to watch and pass an online course on snowmobile operation and safety. A further restriction was that because such trips were possible only by permit, it was a simple matter for park service personnel to simply pull the permit from any group or individual who did not abide by the rules. Only one permit entitling

Cross-country skier par excellence Jenny Wolfe was touring Biscuit Basin on this indescribably beautiful evening on December 20, 2006. The tracks in the foreground were made by snowshoe hares.
JEFF HENRY/ROCHE JAUNE PICTURES, INC.

its holder to independent winter travel through the park was allotted for each of Yellowstone's entrances at any given time.

Another response to growing demand for winter services was the construction of a new Old Faithful Snow Lodge, which first opened for winter operation in the winter of 1998–99. The new building was much more commodious, with interior spaces featuring better design and layout than those of the earlier Snow Lodge. Because of bureaucratic oversight, however, the exterior design of the building was not suited for Yellowstone's winter conditions. The building is in the shape of an "L," with its concave layout on the lee side of the structure, where windblown snow drifts and accumulates. There are also many dormers and architectural valleys on the roof of the new Snow Lodge, and these design features are prone to ice damming and consequent leakage into the interior spaces of the building. Exhaust fans have been added to cool the attic spaces of the building to prevent snow on the roof from melting and then reforming as ice dams, but the fans are noisy, audible for long distances into the Upper Geyser Basin—and in the 1990s and early 2000s noise was one of the issues of contention with regard to older snowmobiles as well as louder models of snowcoaches during the arguments about how Yellowstone should be managed in the winter.

∽

Perhaps the most significant development in Yellowstone in recent years has been the relentless surge in visitation to the park. Since its inception as a park in 1872, visitation to Yellowstone has grown inexorably—the few downturns in visitor

Crystal Cassidy began working in Yellowstone in the summer of 1997 and, as of this writing, is still there today. Crystal drove snowcoaches for many winters, and in this snowy picture she had pulled over to the side of the Grand Loop Road at Gibbon Falls. The snowcoach is a Bombardier, a type that operated in Yellowstone for more than sixty years before being eliminated by the park's principal concessioner in March 2016. JEFF HENRY/ROCHE JAUNE PICTURES, INC.

In a sign of changing times in Yellowstone, this four-wheel-drive van fitted with triangular treads called Mattracks has slid sideways off the road and become hopelessly stuck. Mattracks, in common with several other new innovations for propelling winter vehicles over the snow, are not as reliable as the older caterpillar-type tracks and skis on the original Bombardier coaches. This is especially true in conditions of unpacked and ungroomed snow. In another sign of changing times, the driver of the mired coach is using a cell phone to summon help. JEFF HENRY/ROCHE JAUNE PICTURES, INC.

Lisa Culpepper began working summers in Yellowstone in 2000 and began working winters shortly thereafter. Her first winter driving snowcoaches was 2004–05, and the coach to which Lisa was assigned was nicknamed Little Miss Sunshine, #715. As with most snowcoach drivers, Lisa became very much attached to her assigned coach, and the wetness of Lisa's eyes indicates how much she was saddened when her favorite snowcoach and all the other iconic Bombardiers were sold in March 2016. JEFF HENRY/ROCHE JAUNE PICTURES, INC.

Arden Bailey began his yurt camp at Canyon in the winter of 1983–84 and has worked to improve his operation every winter since then. His lovely camp is set up in a forested site a short distance north of the other developments at Canyon. Arden is shown here taking a break from blowing snow from pathways between the various yurts in his camp—a large kitchen yurt, a larger dining room yurt, and a number of smaller sleeping yurts. Arden also provides snowcoach transportation to and from his Canyon yurt camp, as well as around other snowbound portions of Yellowstone National Park. JEFF HENRY/ ROCHE JAUNE PICTURES, INC.

numbers brought on by major events such as the two world wars and the Great Depression were only temporary, and as soon as the crises cleared, visitation not only rebounded to levels seen before the downturns but also quickly exceeded those earlier numbers. Park visitation hit 3 million for the first time in 2003, then crossed the 4 million threshold just twelve years later. Since 2015 visitation has hovered around the 4 million mark, with the all-time record (for now) set at about 4.25 million in 2016. Even during the coronavirus pandemic year of 2020, when Yellowstone was completely closed from late March until mid-May, and then remained partially closed until June 1, visitation still totaled close to that 4 million figure. Not only was the park closed for much of the spring in 2020, but the pandemic largely eliminated international tourism to Yellowstone, which in recent years has contributed a substantial percentage of visitors to the park's annual count.

Another way to appreciate how Yellowstone's visitation has grown through time and continues to grow at an ever-increasing rate is to consider that it took 121 years for the park to accumulate a total of 100 million visitors. Now, at the rate visitation is progressing, it will welcome its 200 millionth visitor sometime during the year of its 150th anniversary in 2022—only 29 years since the 100 millionth visitor passed through Yellowstone's gates.

The reasons for the swelling flood of visitors are many and include at the most basic level the unrestrained growth of the United States. The country as a whole added around 70 million people between the time Yellowstone hit 3 million annual visitors and the year it reached 4 million. The growing scarcity of wildlife and

A string of pronghorn antelope move across the snowscape near Stephens Creek, near the northern boundary of Yellowstone. Pronghorn antelope were once numerous and widespread across the open plains and prairie country of North America, but by about 1900 they had been eliminated across almost all of their range and survived only in small numbers in protected reserves such as Yellowstone. Overall the species has rebounded in numbers and repopulated much of their range, but the population in Yellowstone remains isolated from other herds of pronghorns and is therefore vulnerable. JEFF HENRY/ROCHE JAUNE PICTURES, INC.

This small group of mule deer was photographed in the Myriad Geyser area behind the Old Faithful Inn on a tremendously cold day in December 1988. A small herd of these deer wintered in the Upper Geyser Basin for decades—historical photos document their winter presence in the geyser basin for more than one hundred years. The number of wintering deer was always small, perhaps ten to twenty at any one time, but they always seemed to persist. That changed in the late 1990s when wolves introduced to the northern reaches of Yellowstone moved as far south as the Firehole geyser basins. Once wolves found this wintering herd of mule deer, it became obvious that the deer could not survive winters in the contained thermal basins. JEFF HENRY/ROCHE JAUNE PICTURES, INC.

Two bull elk feed on an island in the Firehole River shortly before sunset on a beautiful winter evening in Biscuit Basin. Like the mule deer described in the previous photo, the contained thermal basins along the Firehole and other thermally influenced rivers in Yellowstone's interior were not large enough to provide an escape dimension for wintering elk when wolves appeared in the late 1990s and early 2000s. There are virtually no wintering elk in the geyser basins along the Firehole and similar thermal basins today. JEFF HENRY/ROCHE JAUNE PICTURES, INC.

Old Faithful Geyser erupts on a morning when the temperature was nearly 40 degrees below zero. Geyser eruptions at such temperatures are explosive, and the drama and beauty make it easy to understand the attraction of Yellowstone in winter. JEFF HENRY/ROCHE JAUNE PICTURES, INC.

This shot was made right at sunset near Canyon on a cold winter evening, with colors from the setting sun reflecting off the snowpack dotted with the tracks of a pine marten. Again, as in the previous photograph, the beauty and appeal of Yellowstone in winter is clear. JEFF HENRY/ROCHE JAUNE PICTURES, INC.

wild land elsewhere in the country is another factor, a trend that puts more pressure on remaining preserves such as Yellowstone. Another is the growing congestion and pressures of America's increasingly built-out landscapes. A less charitable observation is that many of today's visitors are more motivated to check Yellowstone off their bucket list in a hurried pass-through rather than investing in a longer stay that yields a more in-depth experience—one source recently estimated the average stay in Yellowstone as less than eight hours. It is also worth noting that visitation to Yellowstone is increasing at a rate faster than the pace of national population growth.

The consequences for Yellowstone of this crush of visitors are serious. For one, park roads were not designed to carry the volume of traffic that now traverses them during the summer visitation season. Gridlock often ensues, especially in and near major attractions such as Old Faithful and the Grand Canyon of the Yellowstone. Wildlife sightings near the road are another cause of traffic jams with their predictable frustrations, frayed tempers, and the unpleasantness of motorized din and noxious exhaust fumes. Gridlock also develops in parking areas at roadside attractions and in developed areas, as the number of spaces available is in no way adequate to handle the demand.

Lodging and other visitor facilities are likewise overtaxed by the human tide that engulfs them. Visitors often have to wait in long lines to obtain food or other necessities, and then are further frustrated when they finally reach the head of the line and encounter overwhelmed and exhausted service staff and depleted stocks of goods. Reservations at park hotels and lodges, as well as reservations for campground spaces, are nearly impossible to acquire unless made many months (or even years) in advance. The fundamental infrastructure of the park is often close to the breaking point, where vital systems such as water and sewage treatment operate at maximum capacity. The situation extends to nearly everything—picnic areas, bathrooms, trash and recyclable receptacles, fuel stations, water fountains, boardwalk space from which to view park attractions—everything is pushed to the limit.

The increasing population of the country overall has also led to booming growth in the region surrounding Yellowstone, with major consequences for the park. Communities like Bozeman, Montana, the area around Jackson, Wyoming, and areas in eastern Idaho are among the fastest-growing places in the country. One ominous projection predicts that just the greater Bozeman area will have a population of half a million people by 2050, less than thirty years from now, and most people old enough to remember 1990 agree that was not very long ago, so a date that many years in the future is not very far away. Deteriorating living conditions in many older parts of the country have spurred growth trends in largely rural states like Montana, Wyoming, and Idaho. So has the recent movement toward more and more people working remotely. Among many other considerations, these booming communities put vastly greater numbers of people within a day's drive of the park, and greater levels of visitation, especially in the so-called shoulder seasons of spring and fall, have been a result.

It is interesting that many of today's visitors to Yellowstone are not as put off by the overcrowded conditions as are park employees and managers—to many in today's world the levels of traffic and congestion in the park are minor compared to what they left back home. But park managers especially are concerned about the health of the park itself, as well as the quality of experience for park visitors on their tours. One response by park managers has been to close many areas of the park, including closures for the protection of sensitive species of wildlife and other closures to protect delicate thermal features. Overall, the increased number of visitors has reduced the level of freedom that can be pursued by an individual, a move that is necessary to control crowds and protect the park and its resources.

CHAPTER 10
THE FUTURE

This photograph shows the aftermath of 2003's East Fire, which burned on the east side of Yellowstone Lake and ultimately merged with the Signal Fire to the South. Some of the country in the distance in this photo probably was burned by the Signal Fire. The extent of these joint fires was vast, and the kill of the forest was more or less complete over an extended area. Yellowstone Lake

and snowcapped Mount Sheridan are in the distance. The large island in the lake that can be seen in front of Mount Sheridan is Frank Island. It also burned on August 8, 2003, in a fire separate from the East Fire. JEFF HENRY/ROCHE JAUNE PICTURES, INC.

IN 1977 THE GREAT YELLOWSTONE HIS-TORIAN AUBREY HAINES published his landmark book, *The Yellowstone Story*. The final chapter in his two-volume work was titled "Through a Glass, Darkly," a phrase borrowed from the Bible and in this context meant as an attempt to look into the future. Haines wrote that the future of Yellowstone, as well as the future of the United States, was uncertain and "faced with fearful decisions." From our perspective in the 2020s, it is tempting to discount the concerns that Haines and others had for the future when he wrote those words in the early to mid-1970s. Today, almost fifty years later, we know that both the nation and Yellowstone indeed did survive the immediate future after Haines wrote his milestone history of the park, and that both have continued to survive to the present day. But we must also keep in mind that the worries of

One of the challenges facing Yellowstone Park managers in the years ahead is how to manage ever-increasing levels of visitation. A related problem is the greater degree of isolation of most Americans from the natural world and their consequent lack of knowledge of how to interact with that world when they visit nature preserves such as Yellowstone. Here a large traffic jam and crowd have formed around a mature bull elk near the mouth of Mallard Creek in the Firehole River valley. JEFF HENRY/ROCHE JAUNE PICTURES, INC.

people concerned about the future of Yellowstone in the early to mid-1970s, when the park was observing its 100th anniversary, were as real to them as our concerns for the future are now. And equally obvious is how our own concerns for the future are at least as uncertain for us in these years surrounding Yellowstone's 150th anniversary as were the "fearful decisions" faced by people in the early 1970s.

One of Yellowstone's basic problems is that people love it too much. Soaring rates of visitation, as mentioned in the previous chapter of this book, are having negative impacts on the park's resources. Park infrastructure is overtaxed, and while vast parts of Yellowstone are backcountry areas removed from roads and development and therefore remain lightly visited, the personal experiences of individual visitors at the park's more popular attractions are often diminished by the congestion they encounter. There is something of a paradox here: Because of the restoration of wolves to the ecosystem, and also because of the recovery of a grizzly bear population that had declined to an estimated 136 bears in the early 1970s to a count of more than 700 today, Yellowstone away from the roads is in a sense wilder now that it was in the early 1970s. On the other hand, overcrowding in the developed parts of the park and at its most well-known stops has resulted in a greatly diminished interaction with nature for many visitors.

Many park supporters see a related problem with the brevity of park visits, which at least one source has calculated to be less than eight hours for the average park visitor. The general fast pace of life in today's world is a factor, as is the focus on social media—in the interest of checking items off their lists, it seems that many tourists to Yellowstone make a quick pass-through at points of interest, where they pause only briefly to snap a selfie for posting on social media before hurrying to their next stop. Increasing dependence on technology as a means for viewing existence is regarded as a problem by many who are invested in the natural world. We value what we know and understand, and perceptions of nature that are formed virtually rather than organically may hold less value in building a constituency for the continued preservation of nature reserves like Yellowstone. To a great extent, national parks were created to be a refuge from the confusion and din of the modern world, places where there is time and space for reflection and quiet contemplation. Visitors obsessed with the instant gratification offered by their smartphones are probably not appreciating Yellowstone for the reasons intended by the park's founders.

Overcrowding in national parks is to a great extent a matter of perception based on personal and subjective determinations—a situation that might seem overcrowded to one person might not seem that way at all to someone who has spent his or her life in a major metropolis. But more and more visitors, and especially the large, nationwide

This satellite photo of Yellowstone was taken on August 5, 1987, or just one year prior to the great Yellowstone fires of 1988. In this image of the park, which is only slightly obscured by a small number of clouds, healthy forest appears green while areas lacking dense vegetation for whatever reason appear slightly red. Along the western boundary of the park, for example, there is a clear line of delineation between healthy green forests on the east side of the boundary within the park and the vast clear-cuts of the Targhee National Forest in Idaho on the west side of border, shown as a pale red. Another example is a 1979 fire scar in Tower Creek, which also appears red and is located north of Hayden Valley and southwest of the open Lamar Valley. US GEOLOGICAL SURVEY

This is an image framed similarly to the previous satellite photo, but this one was taken on August 23, 1988, when the Yellowstone fires were in full progress, although they still had another nineteen days to burn before the weather changed and the big burns finally slowed, and during those nineteen days they actually burned much more acreage than they had before. The color scheme in this image is the same as the prior image, with green indicating healthy vegetation and red indicating dead. Smoke is visible from the active burning that was taking place, and the red tracings indicate the country that had already been burned. The largest of the fires within the park was the North Fork Fire, which clearly shows its point of origin from a carelessly discarded cigarette in the Targhee National Forest just outside Yellowstone's west boundary, and then shows with equal clarity the path the fire took as it was blown northeastward by the area's dominant southwesterly winds. US GEOLOGICAL SURVEY

This image was taken about one year after the previous image, during the summer of 1989. The patterns in red show the extensive acreage burned in and around the park in the summer of 1988. These images have been included in this chapter about the future, as they show how much of Yellowstone burned in 1988 and what that might indicate for the future of the park, especially the future of its mature forests, as time goes on and our climate becomes warmer and effectively drier. Many scientists and policy makers now see the 1988 fires as an indication of what will happen in our continually warming world. US GEOLOGICAL SURVEY

bloc of Yellowstone aficionados who are unshakable in their support for the park, see the congestion problem as one that will soon have to be addressed. How to address the problem is, of course, the real problem. Proposals have been made to institute mass transit systems to transport visitors through the park, a move that would necessarily entail the construction of vast parking areas presumably somewhere near the park's entrances. There visitors could leave their automobiles while they tour the park in buses, or perhaps even on monorails in one system that has been suggested and would require a massive construction project. A related problem is that the park and its surrounding ecosystem form an enormous block of roadless country, and since many visit Yellowstone as part of a long-distance or even cross-country trip, having a mass transit system in place at the prohibition of private

Ranger Andrea DeMassi puts up a traffic control sign in a section of Lamar Valley where wolves had consistently been in sight of the road and consequently had been the cause of numerous traffic jams. As visitation to Yellowstone soars, restrictions on individual choices—in this case the opportunity to stop and have a good look at one of the park's most iconic wildlife species—inevitably will become more and more limited.
JEFF HENRY/ROCHE JAUNE PICTURES, INC.

Declining snowpack in Yellowstone will be a continuing and ever-worsening problem in the future. Here National Park Service ranger Wes Miles and volunteer Liz Baker record information on the depth and water content of the snowpack at Canyon, which, gauging from the depth of the snow behind Wes, was very low at the time the photo was taken. JEFF HENRY/ROCHE JAUNE PICTURES, INC.

One consequence of our warming and drying climate that has already occurred is the near elimination of whitebark pines, with the dead skeleton of one shown here standing starkly above a snowbank that has all but disappeared. Whitebark pines grow at high elevations and are adapted to a cold, snowy climate. In recent years winters have not been conducive to whitebark survival, and some estimates now put Yellowstone's population of the species as reduced by 80 to 90 percent. Such trends have a tendency to become self-sustaining and self-accelerating—in the case of dead whitebark pines, the loss of shade they provided while alive further accelerates the melting of snow in the spring. Whitebarks were an extremely important food source for grizzly bears and many other creatures. JEFF HENRY/ROCHE JAUNE PICTURES, INC.

vehicles would necessitate long detours to circumnavigate the region to continue en route to more distant destinations.

Other suggested solutions have included plans to limit visitation by one means or another. Some have even proposed that visitation be limited by increasing entrance fees until they reach a point where some portion of prospective visitors would be deterred. This proposal, of course, does not sit well with many of the values Americans hold dear and hopefully will never be implemented. Other proposals involve using a reservation system (such as the one currently being used in Glacier and Rocky Mountain National Parks), so that only a manageable number of tourists would be

allowed into the park at any one time. A similar proposal would be essentially a first-come, first-served program, where visitors would be allowed through Yellowstone's gates until a daily quota had been met, at which point the gates would be closed and tourists arriving after that time would be turned away and have to find something else to do for the day.

～

Another related problem is the explosive growth of human populations and activities occurring in the greater Yellowstone region. There are dire, but probably realistic, projections that existing nodes of development in the area will grow almost exponentially over just the next couple of decades, to the point where cities like Bozeman, Montana, and Jackson, Wyoming, respectively, will become equivalent in size and population to Minneapolis and Salt Lake City. Similar

In another illustration of the consequences of higher temperatures and drier conditions during Yellowstone's summers, this photograph shows a burned whitebark pine forest high in the Absaroka Mountains above Yellowstone Lake. The lake itself can be seen shining in the distance, behind the small bump in the landscape in front of the lake, which is Lake Butte. This area burned in 2003's East Fire and was not part of the park that burned in 1988, so it is another indication of how fires are burning more frequently, as well as with greater intensity and scope. The East Fire was large, and extensive swaths of forest such as the one pictured here suffered a complete or nearly complete kill. JEFF HENRY/ROCHE JAUNE PICTURES, INC.

predictions have the Big Sky to Ennis area of Montana growing to the size of today's Jackson Hole, and the stretch from Livingston to Gardiner, Montana, at Yellowstone's North Entrance, growing in population to the size of present-day Bozeman. Perhaps most dismaying of all is a prediction that the I-90 corridor between Bozeman and Billings may one day soon have a population of 800,000 to 1 million people (at present the entire population of the state of Montana is only slightly more than 1 million). While estimates of regional growth rates vary, the higher rates will yield the results described above in as little as fifteen to twenty years. It is also worth noting that these projections were made before the great coronavirus pandemic of 2020, a phenomenon that has spurred an exodus from urban areas to more lightly settled areas of the country that city dwellers perceive as offering better quality of life than the more heavily populated places they left behind. This trend is sure to make an impact in the greater Yellowstone area.

The phenomenon of radically accelerating in-migration to the region has profound implications for the future of Yellowstone. Extensive and intensive human development so close to the core of the largest relatively intact ecosystem in the temperate portions of the earth will inevitably sever migration routes for many different species of wildlife. As most of the projected development will occur in the lower-elevation portions of the region, availability of winter range for Yellowstone's famed charismatic megafauna will be substantially diminished. This will exacerbate an underlying problem that has plagued the park since its earliest days: The amount of available winter range, found mostly in lower-elevation country outside the boundaries of the park, is not adequate to balance the amount of excellent summer range available in the higher elevations within Yellowstone National Park. Generally speaking, the challenge will be how to maintain wilderness qualities, including such elements as abundant, free-ranging wildlife and unmarred vistas, with massive human developments in such close proximity. Already it is possible to see the glow in the night sky of Bozeman's city lights from the northern reaches of Yellowstone National Park, an apparition that can be viewed as a gloomy portent of what is to come.

~

Undeniably, Yellowstone's climate is warmer than it was not very long ago. The onset of winter occurs later in the fall, and melt-off of the park's famously deep snowpack comes earlier in the spring. While winter in Yellowstone's interior continues to be characterized as a deep snow environment, and probably will continue to be so for the foreseeable future, the extended periods of deep cold that used to be equally characteristic are now rare to nonexistent. Summers are longer and often dryer than they used to

The young girl shown here peering through a spotting scope was traveling through Yellowstone with her family. In this photo she was looking at distant grizzly bears, but one has to wonder what she will see through her scope when she returns to Yellowstone with her own children or grandchildren.
JEFF HENRY/ROCHE JAUNE PICTURES, INC.

be; consequently the fire season is two months or more longer than it was only a few decades ago. And fires, once started, now have a much wider seasonal window in which to explode to radical intensities and extents. Another telling point is that Yellowstone's forests used to burn only at extended intervals, some of which were as long as two or more centuries. Younger forests simply wouldn't burn, or wouldn't burn much, but in recent years forests aged less than thirty years (that is, since the last time they burned) have gone up in smoke. River flows in late summer often decline to alarmingly low levels, while water temperatures correspondingly rise and so endanger the viability of Yellowstone's famous trout fisheries and the continued existence of the park's native fish and their role in the park's ecosystem.

Changing climate conditions manifest in other negative ways. The pine bark beetle was native to Yellowstone's forests, for example, but in the past, prolonged periods of very cold winter temperatures killed many of the bugs as they tried to survive the winter months inside the bark of pine trees. Today, however, in the absence of sufficiently cold weather, more beetles carry over from one season to the next, and longer summers mean that the bugs have a substantially longer season in which to reproduce. Pine bark beetles are especially hard on Yellowstone's whitebark pines, a species of great importance to grizzly bears and many other species of wildlife. Whitebarks are a species adapted to high-elevation, cold habitats, and so are fundamentally stressed and left vulnerable to a variety of deleterious assaults by the warmer, dryer weather of the changing world. Already as many as 90 percent of Yellowstone's whitebark pine trees have died.

Climate change further damages the ecosystem by making it more vulnerable to invasive, non-native species of both animals and plants. Invasive plants, in particular, have the potential to fundamentally alter Yellowstone's botanical communities on which the park's famous wildlife depends. Many such exotic and damaging species of plants—spotted knapweed being a prime example—have the capacity to create pure stands of just the one species of weed if left unchecked, with the resultant monoculture being unpalatable to native species of grazers. Many such invasive species, including spotted knapweed, are more adapted to lower, warmer, and dryer conditions than most of the habitats found in the interior of Yellowstone National Park, but as climate continues to warm such species may very well find their way to higher, erstwhile cooler portions of the park. And further, it is worth pointing out that pervasive climate change is not a phenomenon that can be fenced out of a preserve like Yellowstone.

Other invasive species, not necessarily related to climate change, are also having widespread impacts on Yellowstone's ecology. Various canine diseases, including distemper, have caused substantial mortalities in Yellowstone's wolf population, and probably in other species of canids as well. The diseases likely originated in dogs kept as pets and spread into the park from outside its boundaries, or perhaps came into the park with dogs whose owners had taken them on vacation. New Zealand mud snails were first detected in the park in 1994, but now have spread to many Yellowstone streams, especially those influenced by geothermal runoff water. In streams where they have established themselves, the mud snails in some cases now constitute as much as 50 percent of the invertebrates present. The problem is that native fish do not find the snails edible, while preferred species of native insects like mayflies and stoneflies that are palatable have had their populations seriously reduced by competition from the snails.

Probably the most damaging invasive species in Yellowstone to date has been the lake trout, which was first discovered in Yellowstone Lake by a fishing guide in 1993 and then confirmed by scientific surveys in 1994. These predatory fish mysteriously appeared in what many of the original explorers described as "a large blue lake on the very top of a mountain," and have decimated the cutthroat trout in what was (until the lake trout appeared) the greatest inland reserve of native cutthroats in the world. A particularly stunning illustration of the cutthroat's decline in Yellowstone Lake is the surveyed number of spawners swimming upstream on Clear Creek, an important spawning stream on the east side of the lake. At a weir near the mouth of Clear Creek, spawning numbers (counted meticulously, one by one by an observer with a clicker counter) peaked at over 70,000 in 1978 but fell to just 538 in 2007. Almost uncountable cascading effects resulted from the reduction of cutthroats, as the species was a food source for a large number of piscivorous predators. The fish, particularly during the bonanza of the spring

Mariah Gale Henry was eighteen months old when this photograph was taken of her looking at bison in Hayden Valley. The future of Yellowstone belongs to the young, and that future will be determined by the attitudes they have toward Yellowstone and similar preserves. Those attitudes, in turn, will be shaped by the experiences they have here, especially while they are young. Hopefully the young will experience the thrills and inspiration that Yellowstone has provided to earlier generations, and the park will continue with all of its wonders intact. JEFF HENRY/ROCHE JAUNE PICTURES, INC.

and early summer spawning season, were an especially important component of the diet of Yellowstone's grizzly bears.

Sustained control efforts aimed at reducing lake trout numbers in Yellowstone Lake have yielded somewhat encouraging results, with the counts of spawning cutthroats in the streams around the lake showing a slight rebound in recent years. Beyond a glimmer of hope regarding the restoration of viable populations of cutthroat trout in Yellowstone Lake and its tributaries, Yellowstone National Park overall remains a beautiful, thrilling, and inspiring place. We can all hope that park managers inside the park, as well as regional managers with local, state, and federal authority on lands around the park, can find ways to manage the park and its surrounding lands that, in the words of the National Park Service Organic Act of 1916, will leave the park and its ecosystem preserved "by such means and measures as . . . to conserve the scenery and the natural and historic objects and the wild life therein and to provide for the enjoyment of the same in such manner and by such means as will leave them unimpaired for the enjoyment of future generations." As Aubrey Haines wrote during the time when Yellowstone was observing its 100th anniversary as a park, we in the 2020s are also facing "fearful decisions" and a doubtful future as we observe the park's 150th anniversary. We can only hope that Yellowstone will survive another fifty years, as it has between Haines's time and ours, and that our children and grandchildren and those who come after them can experience the beauty, thrill, and inspiration of the park for those fifty years and well beyond. As many of the images in this book illustrate, young people are the future of Yellowstone. What they learn about the park, and the values they develop from their experiences here, will determine how the park fares through the rest of the next fifty years and beyond.

ACKNOWLEDGMENTS

WHEN I FIRST CAME TO YELLOWSTONE, I found it a beautiful and exciting place, as I knew it would be from the books and maps I had studied beginning pretty much as soon as I could read. For me Yellowstone is still a beautiful place, but that place is now an interwoven fabric of countless memories of thrilling, inspiring experiences I have been fortunate enough to have had here, and also the memories of the people with whom I had those experiences. It's still the place, but also the experiences and the people, all blended into one marbled mix.

In a very real sense I began collecting information for this book as soon as I arrived to take my first job in Yellowstone on May 25, 1977. Therefore, I would like to acknowledge the people who helped me at each stage of my Yellowstone career. Many of the names below are of people who are no longer living, and so my expressions of gratitude will not reach them. My hope is that there are still living friends and relatives of those people who have passed, and that the living will see this list and understand how much I appreciated the help and friendship of those who are gone. Living and passed, I hereby offer a sincere thank you to all the people listed in the acknowledgments below.

For my time as a fishing guide on Yellowstone Lake, working out of Bridge Bay Marina, I would like to thank Jeff Mosier, Karl Bittler, Tom Hansen, Rick "R. B." and Kathy Braune, Kate and Ron "Conan" Wilson, Joel Henry, Phil Cooper, Lyle Benefiel, Johnny Blair, Neil Rowe.

For the years I spent working as a maintenance man, heavy laborer, and truck driver for the Engineering Division of the Yellowstone Park Company, as well as a short time for its successors, I would like to thank Dallas Proffit, Todd King, Jim Peaco, Jeff Olson, Herb Majerus, Mark Hargis, Chuck Wyman, George Swim, Gary Durfey.

The jobs I had working for the Interagency Grizzly Bear Study Team brought some of the best experiences I have ever had. For those experiences and for what I learned from them, I thank Dave Mattson, Mark Haroldson, Kerry Gunther, Gerry Greene, Steve and Marilyn French, Jamie Jonkel along with Jamie's parents Chuck and Joan Jonkel, Dan Reinhart, Kevin Frey.

For my time working as a park ranger, I thank John Lounsbury, Mark Marschall, Mona Devine, Les Inafuku, Jim Sweeney, Joe Fowler, Sandi Fowler, Rick Hutchinson, Dan Krapf, Bob Mahn, Jennifer Whipple, Gary "Dub" Kennedy, Rick Bennett, Les Brunton, Bob Duff, Bob Jackson.

For my time working on a coyote research project on Yellowstone's famed Northern Range, I thank Bob Crabtree, John Shivik, Brian Kelly, Greg "Zip" Zoppetti, Craig Perham, Pat Terletsky, Eric Gese, Minette Johnson, Scott Relyea.

Without any question winterkeeping in Yellowstone has been my passion for more than forty years, and thus has been the best job I have ever had. I want to thank Patrick Povah, Herb Vaughn, Bill Berg, Steve Fuller, Bill Powell, Jerry Bateson Sr., Gerry Bateson Jr., Cliff Hartman, Dan Beadle, Dale Fowler, Jim McBride, Chuck McNabb, Jenny Wolfe, Ron Wilkes, Erin Benicke, Jason Fatourous, Lou Smith, Holt Rawlings, Pete Donau, Derek Zwickey, Derek Johnston, Jeff Guengrich, Hal Broadhead.

For the many years I spent shooting photographs, researching Yellowstone history, and writing articles and books, I would like to thank Jim Peaco, Aubrey Haines, Tim Daly, Jackie Jerla, Jerry Brekke, Larry Lahren, George Bornemann, Leslie and Ruth Quinn, and especially Lee Whittlesey, retired official historian of Yellowstone National Park and the undisputed dean of Yellowstone history.

For general Yellowstone friendships not related to employment in the park, I want to thank Mark "Doc" Watson, Mike Bryers, Kathryn Bornemann, Derek Johnston, Mark Ringo, James Malone, Clark and Monica Baumgarz, Kevin Gilbert, Lisa Culpepper, Crystal Cassidy, Steve Blakeley, Louise Mercier, and Connie Dover. I also want to thank Arden Bailey and Erica Hudgings of Yellowstone Expeditions in West Yellowstone, Montana, for their friendship and for the countless times they rendered practical aid for my mechanical breakdowns and other mishaps. And there are many others.

Specific thanks with regard to this book project are due to Rick Rinehart, executive editor at Lyons Press; James and Lynne Bama for their friendship and for allowing me to use some of James's superb art; Gary and Marlys Carter for decades of friendship and for permission to use some of Gary's signature paintings of Yellowstone subjects; Mike Bryers for his friendship and his fine artwork depicting historical scenes in Yellowstone; Bob Smith for sharing some of his wealth of information regarding Yellowstone geology and also allowing me to use some of his academic illustrations; Eric Boyd for his friendship and also for furnishing me with a photograph of his geothermal research work in Yellowstone; Andrew W. Weiland, PhD, Cultural Resources Program manager at Hopewell Culture National Historical Park in Chillicothe, Ohio, for photographing the exquisite artifacts in that park's collection that were wrought centuries ago from Yellowstone obsidian; Todd Fredricksen for his friendship and for allowing me to use his powerful art; Doug Smith of the Yellowstone Wolf Project for his friendship and for providing me with photographs of his work; Jim Peaco, official photographer for Yellowstone National Park and one of the world's nicest guys, for

helping me find certain photographs relating to the park's history, and for further supplying me with information about the same; Cam Sholly, superintendent of Yellowstone National Park, for cutting through bureaucratic red tape to allow me to use certain illustrations in this book; Erin White, a hydrologist for Yellowstone National Park, for furnishing me photographs of herself at work in the park; Jackie Jerla of the Yellowstone National Park archives for helping me countless times with research into the park's history and other subjects; and Lee Whittlesey for his unflagging willingness to share his wealth of knowledge regarding the history of Yellowstone, and also for writing the foreword to this book.

ABOUT THE AUTHOR

JEFF HENRY WAS BORN IN NORTHERN PENNSYLVANIA BUT HAS LIVED his entire adult life in or near Yellowstone National Park in southern Montana and northern Wyoming. He has worked various jobs in and around Yellowstone Park for the past forty-five years, including as a fishing guide, wildlife researcher, tour guide, resource manager, park ranger, and winterkeeper of the park's lodges. He is the author and photographer of *Survive: Snow Country* (FalconGuides, 2016), *The Year Yellowstone Burned* (Taylor, 2015), *The Yellowstone Winter Guide* (Roberts Rinehart, 1993), *Snowshoes, Coaches and Cross Country Skis: A Brief History of Yellowstone Winters* (Roche Jaune Pictures, 2010), as well as nearly a dozen other books he has produced, some on his own and others in conjunction with other authors. Jeff lives in a log house of his own construction on the banks of the Yellowstone River just a few miles north of Yellowstone National Park, and still works winters in the park as a roof shoveler and winterkeeper for Yellowstone General Stores and Yellowstone Forever.